Summer Activities

Grow Your Brain

D1573159

About Me!

Write your name.

_____

_____

Date

_____

Hey! Paste your picture here!

Age?

Greatness!

In this oval, write something that is great about you!

_____

_____

_____

Where do you live?

Your city _____

Your state _____

Who is your best friend?

My best friend is:

_____

Top 5 Vacation Spots

List the top 5 places that you would like to visit.

_____

_____

_____

_____

_____

Kindergarten to First Grade

Copyright © 2005 Cookie Jar Publishing

All rights reserved.

ISBN: 1-594413-22-3

PRINTED IN THE UNITED STATES OF AMERICA
10 9 8 7 6 5 4 3 2 1

What's Inside!

Parent Letter...iv

How to Use **Summer Activities**..v

Encourage Your Child to Read..vi

Reading Book List...vii

Ready for Reading 1

Try Something New 2

Activities in Math, Reading, Writing, and Language Arts 3

Summer Fun 33

Try Something New..34

Activities in Math, Reading, Writing, and Language Arts 35

Summer Fun 75

Try Something New..76

Activities in Math, Reading, Writing, and Language Arts 77

Answer Pages 107

Hey Kids,

Can you believe that summer is already here? Think of all the time playing at the pool and hanging out at park, going to baseball games and staying up late, not to mention the family barbeques, Fourth of July fireworks, and of course spending all that time hanging out with your pals. But wait we need to add one more thing—this book!

With all the fun of summer, it's sometimes easy to forget that the new school year (sorry!) is waiting for us, and if summer is all play and no brain activity, then going back to school may not be nearly as fun as it should be!

So to help this be one of the most favorite, most exciting, most memorable summers on record, we came up with a really cool and easy way to help you remember all the great things you learned in reading, math, and writing last year so you are primed and ready to go on the first day of school next year! It's easy to use, and don't worry, we made sure that the activities are fun, interesting, and, of course, short! That way you will be done in no time and off to your next big adventure!

Have fun and enjoy everything you do this summer, and of course, remember to use your sunscreen, look out after your brothers and sisters, don't eat too many hot dogs at the barbecue, and above all, don't forget this book! Have a great summer!

The Cookie Jar Kids Club

How to Use  Summer Activities

 First, let your child explore the book. Flip through the pages and look at the activities with your child to help him/her become familiar with the book.

 Help select a good time for reading or working on the activities. Suggest a time before your child has played outside and becomes too tired to do their work.

 Provide any necessary materials. A pencil, ruler, eraser, and crayons are all that are required.

 Offer positive guidance. Children need a great deal of guidance. Remember, the activities are not meant to be tests. You want to create a relaxed and positive attitude toward learning. Work through at least one example on each page with your child. "Think aloud" and show your child how to solve problems.

 Give your child plenty of time to think. You may be surprised by how much children can do on their own.

 Stretch your child's thinking beyond the page. If you are reading a storybook, you might ask, "What do you think will happen next?" or "What would you do if this happened to you?" Encourage your child to name objects that begin with certain letters, or count the number of items in your shopping cart. Also, children often enjoy making up their own stories with illustrations.

 Reread stories and occasionally flip through completed pages. Completed pages and books will be a source of pride to your child and will help show how much he/she accomplished over the summer.

 Read and work on activities while outside. Take the workbook out in the backyard, to the park, or to a family campout. It can be fun wherever you are!

 Encourage siblings, babysitters, and neighborhood children to help with reading and activities. Other children are often perfect for providing the one-on-one attention necessary to reinforce reading skills.

 Give plenty of approval! Stickers and stamps, or even a hand-drawn funny face, are effective for recognizing a job well done. At the end of the summer, your child can feel proud of his/her accomplishments and will be eager for school to start.

Reading is the primary means to all learning. If a child cannot read effectively, other classroom subjects can remain out of reach.

You were probably the first person to introduce your child to the wonderful world of reading. As your child grows, it is important to continue encouraging his/her interest in reading to support the skills they are being taught in school.

This summer, make reading a priority in your household. Set aside time each day to read aloud to your child at bedtime or after lunch or dinner. Encourage your child take a break from playing, and stretch out with a book found on the **Summer Activities** Reading Book List. Choose a title that you have never read, or introduce your child to some of the books you enjoyed when you were their age! Books only seem to get better with time!

Visit the library to find books that meet your child's specific interests. Ask a librarian which books are popular among children of your child's grade. Take advantage of summer storytelling activities at the library. Ask the librarian about other resources, such as stories on cassette, compact disc, and the Internet.

Encourage reading in all settings and daily activities. Encourage your child to read house numbers, street signs, window banners, and packaging labels. Encourage your child to tell stories using pictures.

Best of all, show your child how much YOU like to read! Sit down with your child when he/she reads and enjoy a good book yourself. After dinner, share stories and ideas from newspapers and magazines that might interest your child. Make reading a way of life this summer!

Easy Readers

Galdone, Paul
Little Red Hen

Gregorich, Barbara
The Fox on the Box

Hillert, Margaret
A House for Little Red
Circus Fun
Dear Dragon books
Little Puff
The Cookie House
The Funny Baby
The Three Bears

Hoff, Syd
Danny and the Dinosaur

Schade, Susan and Jon Buller
Cat on the Mat

Seuss, Dr.
The Cat in the Hat
Fox In Socks
Green Eggs and Ham
One Fish, Two Fish,
Red Fish, Blue Fish

Modern Curriculum Press
Max series

Modern Curriculum Press
Set 1—Short Vowels
Fun with Gus
Gus
Hop On, Hop Off
Hot Rocks
Jet Bed
Jim Wins
Max
Red Hen
Sam and Al
Six Kids

Modern Curriculum Press
Set 2—Long Vowels
Bike Hike
Dave and his Raft
Dune Bug
I Like What I Am
Joe and Moe
Katie and Jake
Mr. Jones and Mr. Bones
Pete and his Beans
Sue and June
Zeke

Modern Curriculum Press
Set 3—Blends
At the Pond
Brag, Brag, Brag
Glen Wit
Glub, Glub
Here Comes the Bride
Hunk of Junk
Miss Swiss
Scat, Cat
Squire's Square Deal
Stan the Squid

Modern Curriculum Press
Set 4—Digraphs
At the Beach
Bath Time
Black Ducks Wind Ding
Gretch the Witch
Jack's King
Mush? Mush!
Sh!
Smith's Store
The White Whale
Whiz Kid

Books To Read to Children

Andersen, Hans Christian
Snow Queen

Berenstain, Stan & Jan
The Berenstain Bears series

Blishen, Edward
Oxford Book of Poetry for
Children

Bridwell, Norman
Clifford the Big Red Dog series

Butterworth, Oliver
Enormous Egg

Cleary, Beverly
Ramona the Pest

Dahl, Roald
Enormous Crocodile
Fantastic Mr. Fox

Dorros, Arthur
Follow the Water From Brook
to Ocean

Duvoisin, Roger
Petunia

Gibbons, Gail
New Road!
Trucks
The Puffins are Back

Hawes, Judy
Fireflies in the Night

Jordan, Helene J.
How A Seed Grows

Joyce, William
Bently and Egg

MacDonald, Betty
Mrs. Piggle Wiggle

Mauser, Pat Rhodes
Patti's Pet Gorilla

Milne, A.A.
Winnie the Pooh

Numeroff, Laura Joffe
If You Give A Mouse A Cookie
If You Give A Moose A Muffin

Parish, Peggy
Amelia Bedelia books

Prelutsky
Random House of Poetry for
Children

Sendak, Maurice
Where the Wild Things Are
Outside Over There
In the Night Kitchen

Stevenson, Robert Lewis
A Child's Garden of Verse

Thurber, James
Many Moons

Ward, Lynd
The Biggest Bear

Warner, Gertrude
The Boxcar Children

Williams, Margery
Velveteen Rabbit

Happy Reading!

Ready for Reading

✔ Reading has been around for thousands of years and can open your mind to new ideas by making you think in different ways than television or radio!

✔ The more you read, the smarter you get!

Books I Have Finished Reading

Title	Author	Pages	Date Finished	Great	Evaluation Okay	Bad

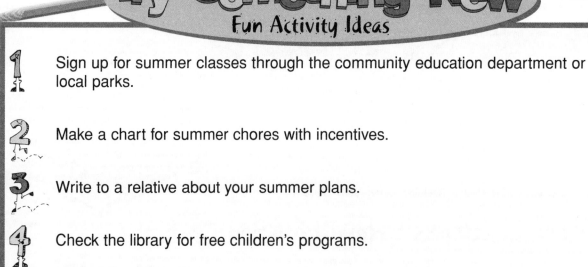

Try Something New
Fun Activity Ideas

1 Sign up for summer classes through the community education department or local parks.

2 Make a chart for summer chores with incentives.

3 Write to a relative about your summer plans.

4 Check the library for free children's programs.

5 Boost reading—make labels for household objects.

6 Start a journal of summer fun.

7 Have a zoo contest—find the most African animals.

8 Shop together—use a calculator to compare prices.

9 Tune up those bikes. Wash 'em, too.

10 Play flashlight tag.

11 Check out a science book—try some experiments.

12 Make up a story at dinner. Each person adds a new paragraph.

13 Enjoy the summer solstice. Time the sunrise and sunset.

14 Have some bubble fun: one-third cup liquid dishwashing soap, plus two quarts water. Use cans or pipe cleaners for dippers.

15 Arrange photo albums.

When using a pencil, REMEMBER to:

1. Hold your pencil correctly.

2. Sit up straight with both feet flat on the floor.

3. Make your letters with even circles, curves, and straight lines.

4. Space the letters in your words evenly.

5. Space your words evenly on the line.

6. Make your writing neat and easy to read.

7. Practice writing quickly as well as neatly.

8. Some people write right-handed and other people write left-handed.

Left-handed

Right-handed

The thumb and first finger form a good "o."
The middle finger supports the pencil.
A good position helps make good writing habits.

Say the alphabet in order, then choose a letter and say it aloud. Make sure you know the difference between capital and lowercase letters.

Aa Bb Cc
Dd Ee Ff Gg
Hh Ii Jj Kk
Ll Mm Nn Oo
Pp Qq Rr Ss
Tt Uu Vv Ww
Xx Yy Zz

Another fun thing to do is to have an adult in your family say a letter, then you find it and put a marker on it (a button, bean, etc.). Continue this until you have covered all the letters.

Writing numbers can be fun. Remember to always write your numbers beginning at the top.

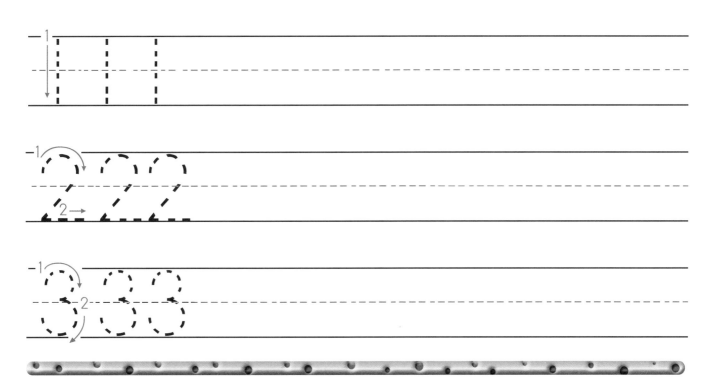

Color the fish green, the octopus orange, and the whale blue. Trace the path in the same color to help the sea creatures find their way home.

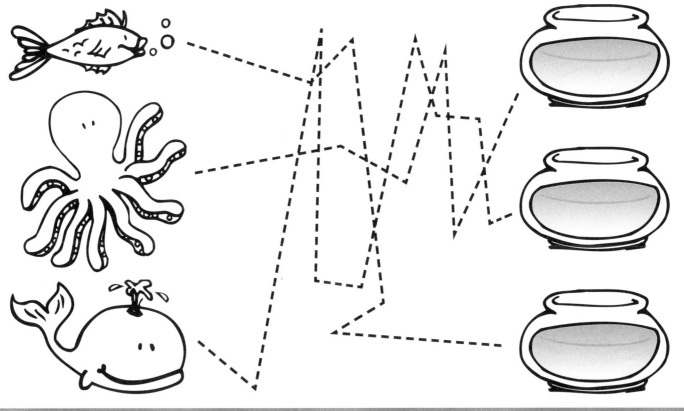

COOKIE JAR PUBLISHING

Bat and ball begin with the sound of (b). Practice writing capital and lowercase (b's).

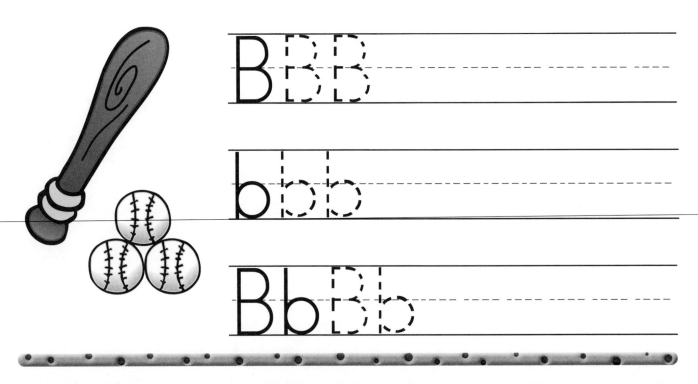

B B B

b b b

B b B b

Now color all the objects below that begin with the sound of (b), like bat and ball.

Writing numbers can be fun. Remember to always write your numbers beginning at the top.

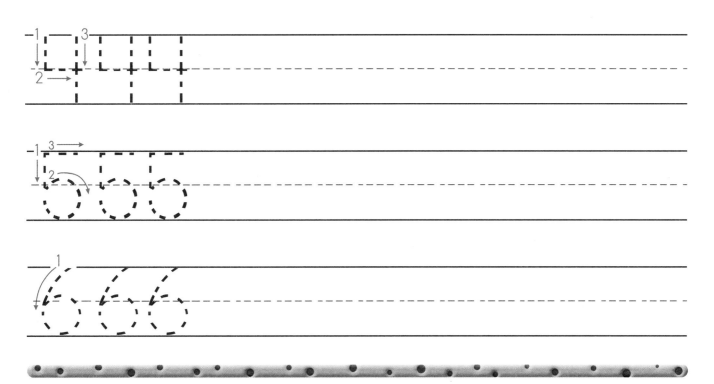

Circle the shape that is different in each box.

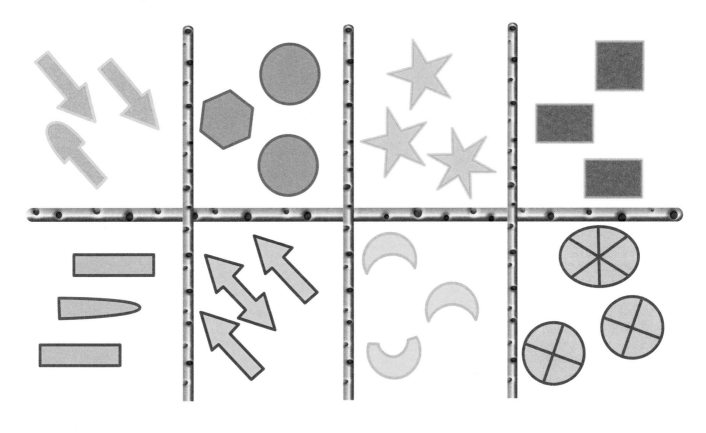

Carrots begin with the sound of (c). Practice writing capital and lowercase (c's).

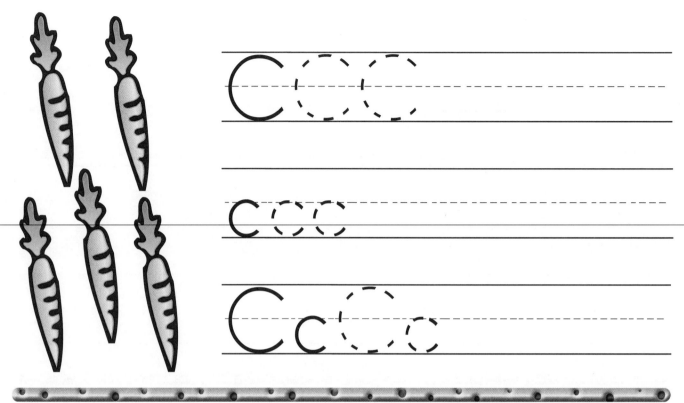

Now color all the objects below that begin with the sound of (c), like carrot.

1, 2, 3, 4, 5, 6, we are not ready to quit! Now try numbers 7, 8, and 9.
Remember to write your numbers beginning at the top.

Make each picture look exactly the same as the first one in each row.

Duck begins with the sound of (d). Practice writing capital and lowercase (d's).

Now color all the objects below that begin with the sound of (d), like duck.

Color the number of squares to match the number at the beginning of each row.

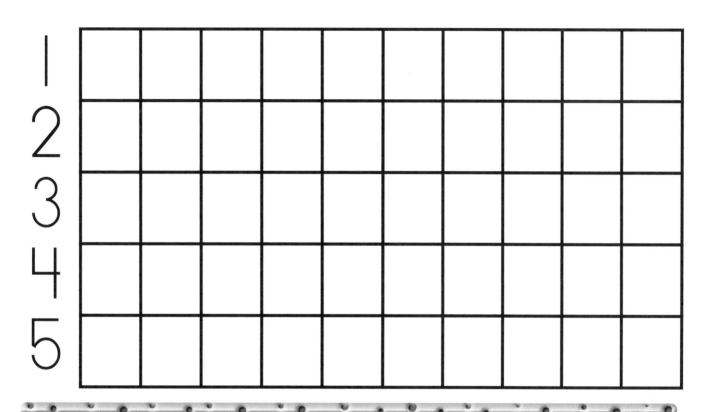

Trace over each capital letter.

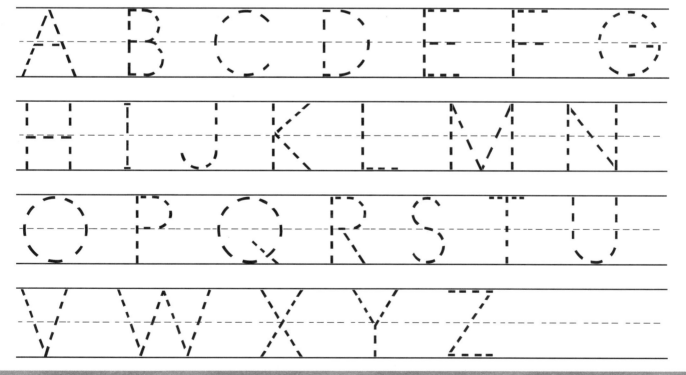

Fish begins with the sound of (f). Practice writing capital and lowercase (f's).

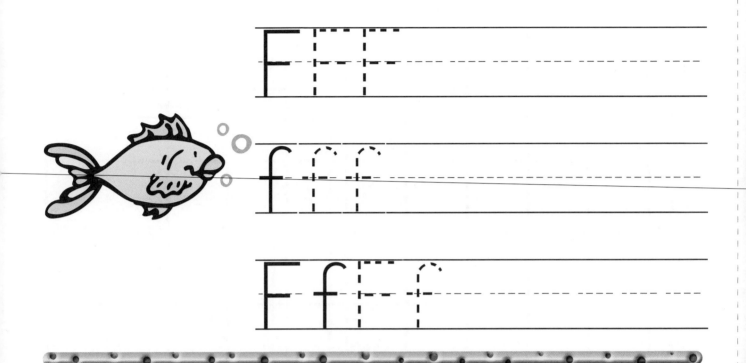

Now color all the objects below that begin with the sound of (f), like fish.

Color the number of squares to match the number at the beginning of each row.

6										
7										
8										
9										
10										

Write the missing lowercase letters in their boxes.

a	b			e		g
	i		k			n
o		q				u
v				z		

Girl begins with the sound of (g). Practice writing capital and lowercase (g's).

Now color all the objects that begin with the sound of (g), like girl.

Write the number telling how many objects are in each box.

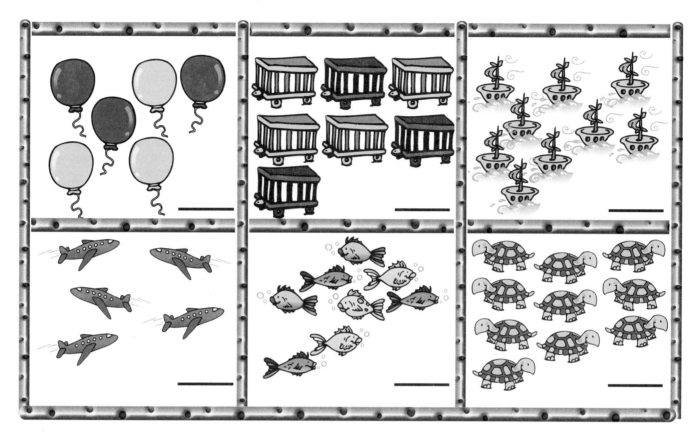

Write the missing capital letters in their boxes.

A	B			E	
H					M
		Q		S	
	W			Z	

COOKIE JAR PUBLISHING

Horse begins with the sound of (h). Practice writing capital and lowercase (h's).

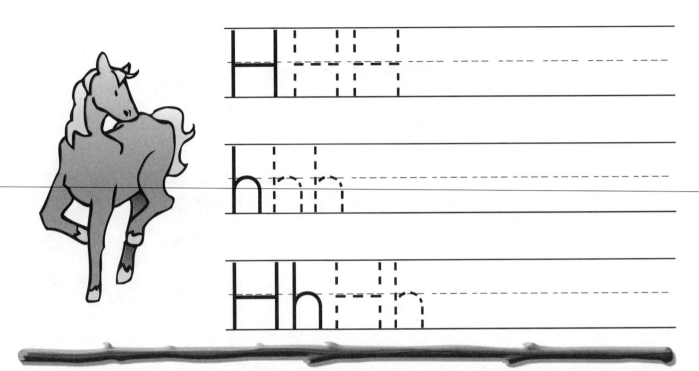

Now color all the objects below that begin with the sound of (h), like horse.

Color the butterfly by matching the number of dots in each shape to the numbered crayon.

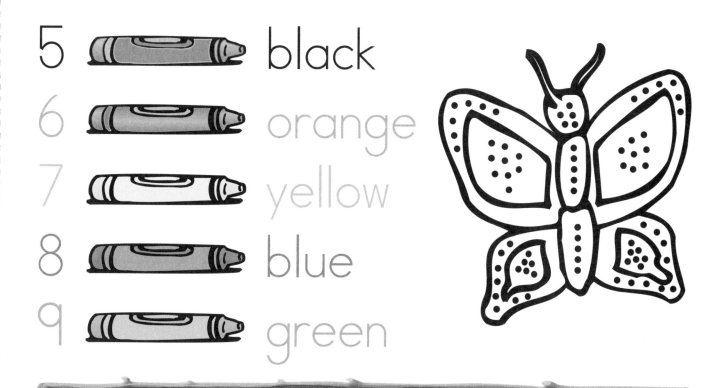

5   black

6   orange

7   yellow

8   blue

9   green

Complete the pattern in each row.

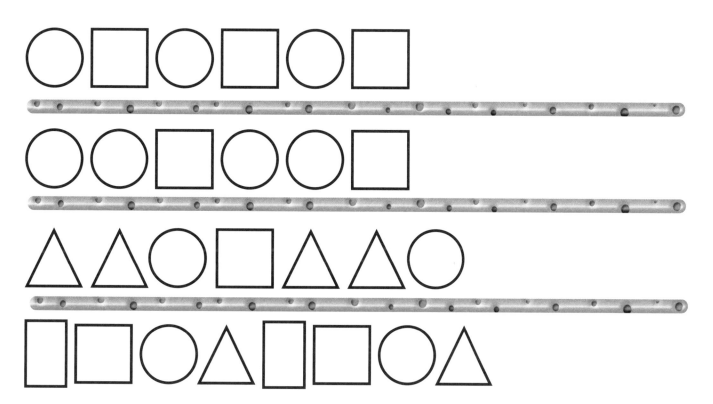

Jug begins with the sound of (j). Practice writing capital and lowercase (j's).

Now color all the objects that begin with the sound of (j), like jug.

In each box, draw and color as many objects as the number shows.

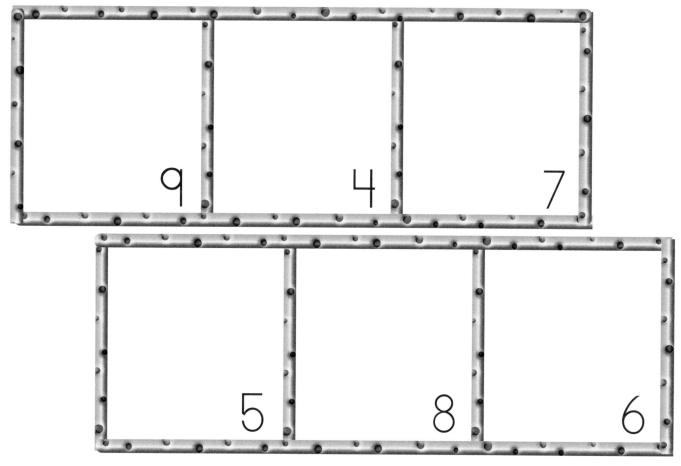

9   4   7

5   8   6

Draw a line from the capital letter to the matching lowercase letter.

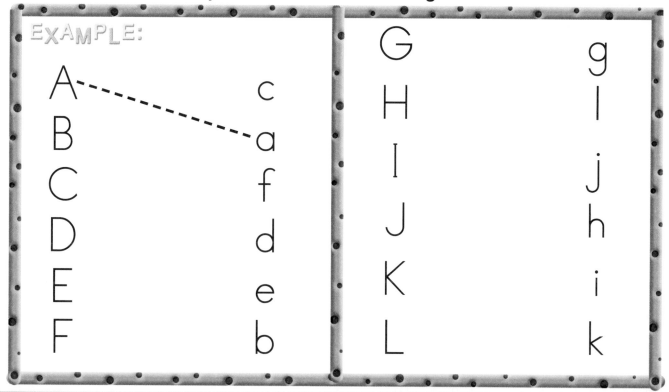

EXAMPLE:

A   c
B   a
C   f
D   d
E   e
F   b

G   g
H   l
I   j
J   h
K   i
L   k

Kangaroo begins with the sound of (k). Practice writing capital and lowercase (k's).

Now color all the objects below that begin with the sound of (k), like kangaroo.

Help Mother Bird lay the right amount of eggs. Draw and color as many eggs in each nest as the number shows.

Draw a line from the capital letter to the matching lowercase letter.

EXAMPLE:

M - - - - - - - - - - - - - m

N
O
P
Q
R
S

p
q
r
s
n
o

T
U
V
W
X
Y
Z

u
t
v
x
z
y
w

Lion begins with the sound of (l). Practice writing capital and lowercase (l's).

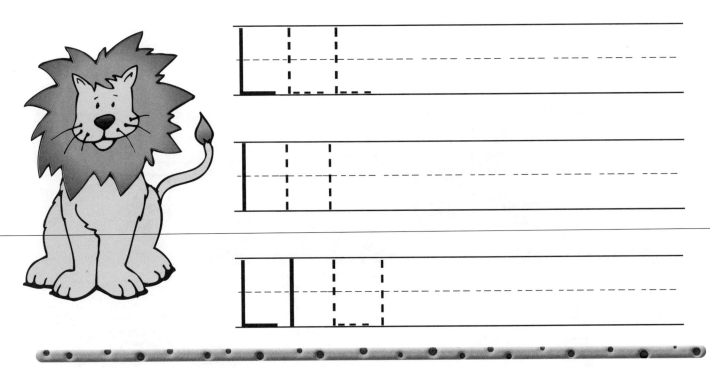

Now color all the objects below that begin with the sound of (l), like lion.

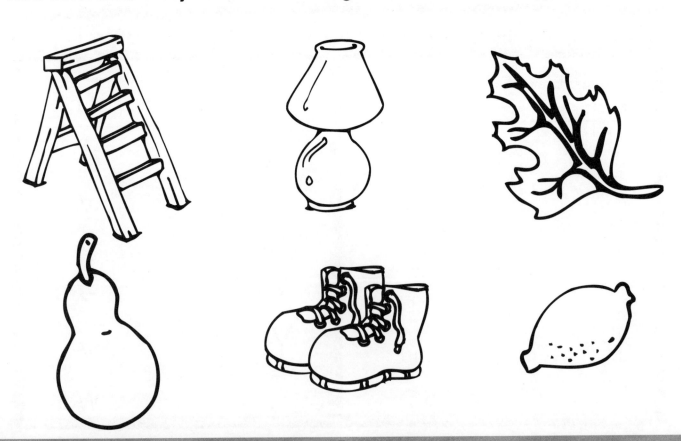

Write the number that comes next.

1 2 3 4 5 6 __ __ __

5 6 7 8 __ __ 11

0 1 2 3 4 __ __ __ __

8 9 10 11 12 __ __ __

16 17 18 __ __ 21

Color the letters green and the numbers blue.

8 w n c v

i p m l 7

h 5 r 3 b

t a k x 2

Mouse begins with the sound of (m). Practice writing capital and lowercase (m's).

Now color all the objects below that begin with the sound of (m), like mouse.

Count the blocks and write the number in the blank provided.

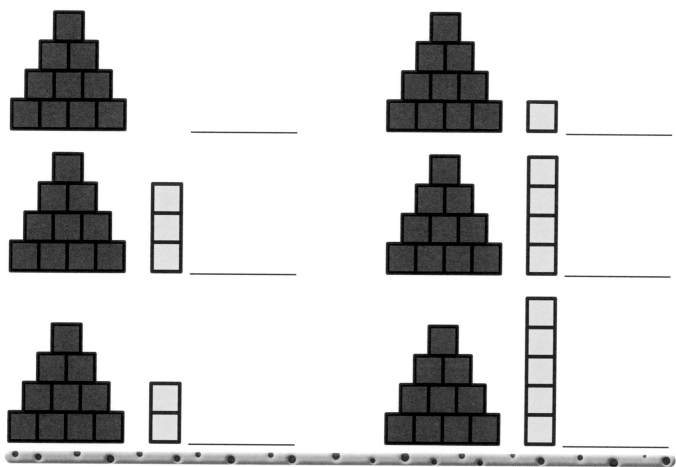

_____   _____

_____   _____

_____   _____

Color the stars with matching capital and lowercase letters in them.

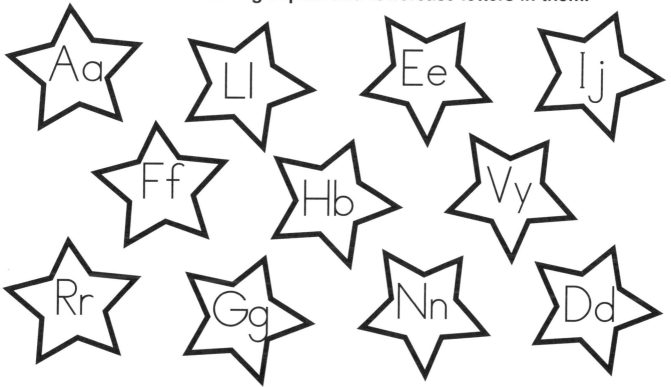

Nurse begins with the sound of (n). Practice writing capital and lowercase (n's).

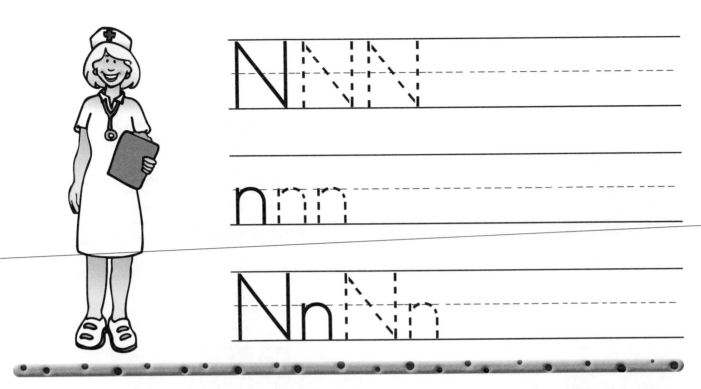

Now color all the objects below that begin with the sound of (n), like nurse.

Draw and color.

Draw 9 apples in the tree.

Draw 3  nests in the tree.

Draw 1 bird in the tree and 4 more birds flying.

Draw 7 flowers and color your picture.

How many objects did you draw in all?

_____

Write the capital letter on the blank line that follows each letter in the alphabet.

EXAMPLE:

A B   K L   C __   X __

Q __   E __   N __   L __

G __   F __   I __   O __

D __   H __   S __   Y __

Peanut begins with the sound of (p). Practice writing capital and lowercase (p's).

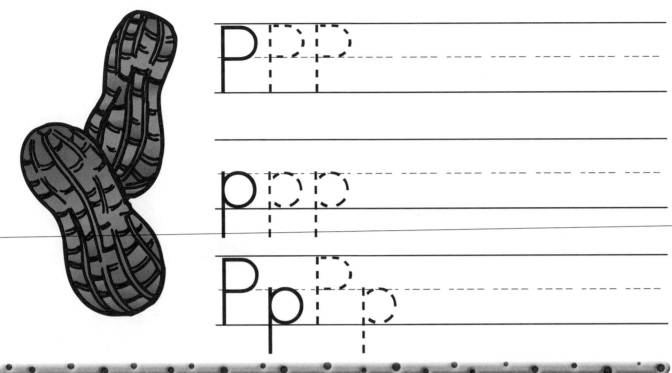

Now color all the objects below that begin with the sound of (p), like peanut.

Write the missing numbers.

1 2 3 4 ___ 6 7 ___

9 10 ___ 12 ___ 14 15

16 ___ ___ 19 20 21 ___

23 24 ___ 26 ___ ___ 29

30 31 ___ 33 ___ ___ 36

Draw the faces in each row that come next to finish the pattern.

Queen begins with the sound of (q). Practice writing capital and lowercase (q's).

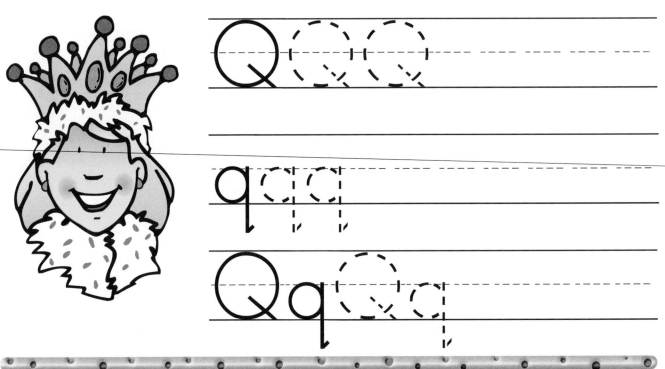

Now color all the objects below that begin with the sound of (q), like queen.

Write the numbers 1 to 25 in the empty boxes.

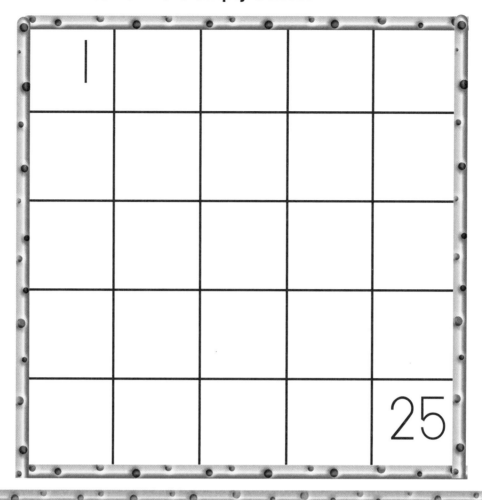

Finish drawing the other half of the pictures.

ice cream cone

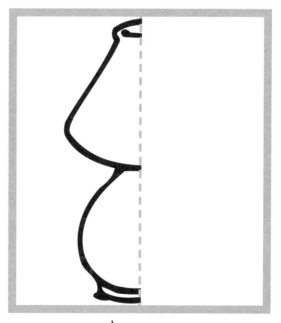

lamp

Ruler begins with the sound of (r). Practice writing capital and lowercase (r's).

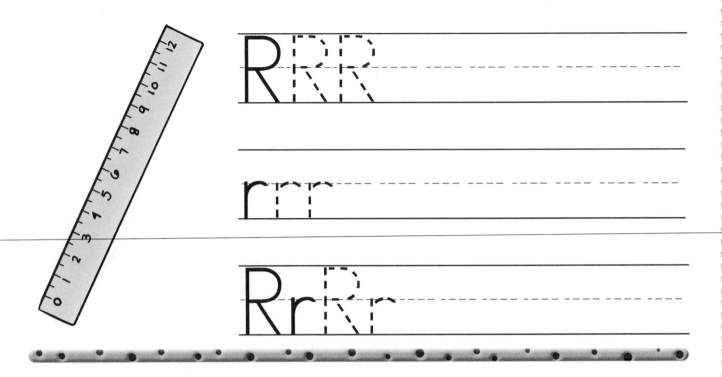

Now color all the objects below that begin with the sound of (r), like ruler.

Homemade Ice Cream

Make homemade ice cream with your favorite frozen fruit or flavor . . . vanilla, chocolate, etc.

1 cup whole milk	1/4 cup rock salt
1 gallon ziplock bag	4 tablespoons sugar
3 - 4 cups crushed ice	1 quart ziplock bag
1/4 teaspoon vanilla	frozen fruit or flavor

2 whole sheets of newspaper
duct tape

In the small bag, mix milk, vanilla, sugar, and fruit or flavor. Squeeze out the air and close the bag. Place the small bag inside the large bag. Add the ice and salt to the large bag. Remove the air and close the bag. Wrap in 2 sheets of newspaper, tape with duct tape. Shake for 10 minutes.

Pasta Cards

Use dry, uncooked macaroni noodles to decorate cards. Glue the noodles to colored construction paper and let dry.

Paint or color with markers to decorate. You can make cards for all occasions.

Try Something New
Fun Activity Ideas

1. Decorate your bike. Have a neighborhood parade.

2. Catch a butterfly.

3. Get the neighborhood together and play hide-and-seek.

4. Take a tour of the local hospital.

5. Check on how your garden is doing.

6. Make snow cones with crushed ice and punch.

7. Go on a bike ride.

8. Run through the sprinklers.

9. Create a family symphony with bottles, pans, and rubber bands.

10. Collect sticks and mud. Build a bird's nest.

11. Help plan your family grocery list.

12. Go swimming with a friend.

13. Clean your bedroom and closet.

14. Go to the local zoo.

15. In the early morning, listen to the birds sing.

16. Make a cereal treat.

17. Read a story to a younger child.

18. Lie down on the grass and find shapes in the clouds.

19. Color noodles with food coloring. String them for a necklace or glue a design on paper.

20. Organize your toys.

**Finish writing the numbers on the clock. Color the (big) minute hand red.
Color the (small) hour hand blue.**

Trace and color the words and pictures with the matching crayon color.

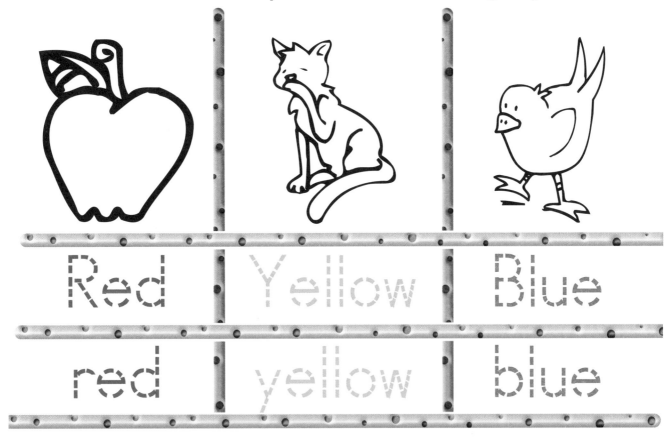

Red | Yellow | Blue

red | yellow | blue

COOKIE JAR PUBLISHING

Sandwich begins with the sound of (s). Practice writing capital and lowercase (s's).

Now color all the objects below that begin with the sound of (s), like sandwich.

Trace the numbers on the clock. Draw minute and hour hands so the clocks show the correct time. Color the minute hand red. Color the hour hand blue.

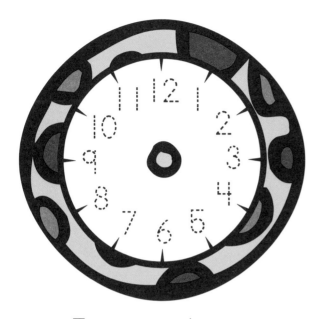

Time to wake up.

Time to go to bed.

Trace and color the words and pictures with the matching crayon color.

COOKIE JAR PUBLISHING

Table begins with the sound of (t). Practice writing capital and lowercase (t's).

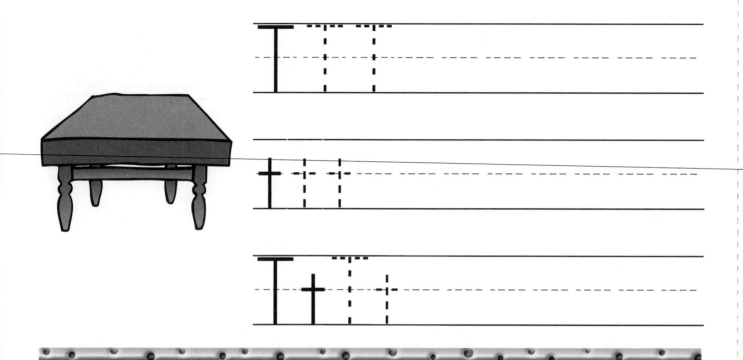

Now color all the objects below that begin with the sound of (t), like table.

What time is it? Look at each clock and write the time it shows.

_____:_____

_____:_____

_____:_____

Trace and color the words and pictures with the matching crayon color.

Brown   Violet   Black

brown   violet   black

Valentine begins with the sound of (v). Practice writing capital and lowercase (v's).

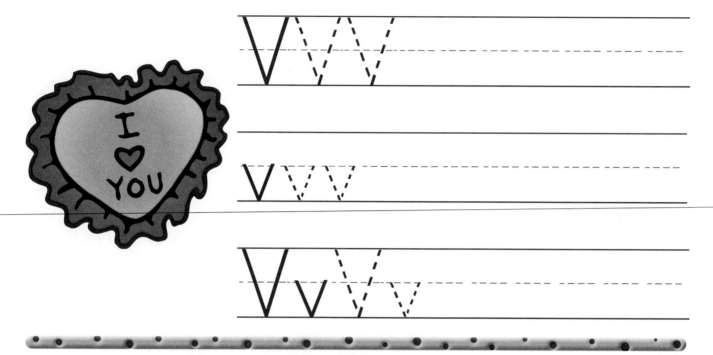

Now color all the objects below that begin with the sound of (v), like valentine.

How many beans are in the pot?
Materials needed: Beans for counting. Put the amount of beans in the pot for each problem, then count to see how many you have altogether!

$$\begin{array}{r} 1 \\ +\,1 \\ \hline \end{array} \qquad \begin{array}{r} 2 \\ +\,2 \\ \hline \end{array} \qquad \begin{array}{r} 1 \\ +\,2 \\ \hline \end{array} \qquad \begin{array}{r} 3 \\ +\,1 \\ \hline \end{array}$$

$$\begin{array}{r} 2 \\ +\,1 \\ \hline \end{array} \qquad \begin{array}{r} 3 \\ +\,2 \\ \hline \end{array} \qquad \begin{array}{r} 1 \\ +\,3 \\ \hline \end{array} \qquad \begin{array}{r} 2 \\ +\,3 \\ \hline \end{array}$$

Color the fish in the fishbowl.

Watermelon begins with the sound of (w). Practice writing capital and lowercase (w's).

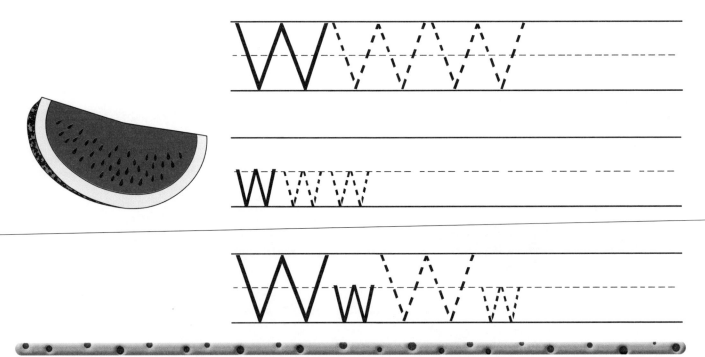

Now color all the objects below that begin with the sound of (w), like watermelon.

1. Color the bowl with less fish in it.

2. Color the pan that has more cookies in it.

Take the mouse to his cheese.

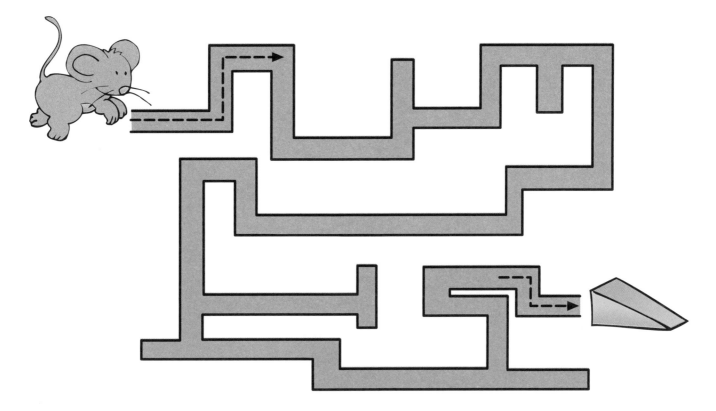

X-ray begins with the sound of (x). Practice writing capital and lowercase (x's).

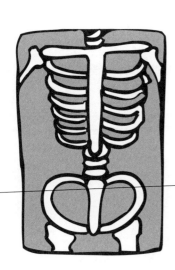

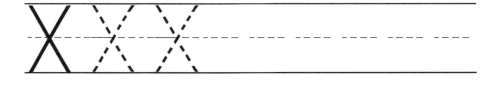

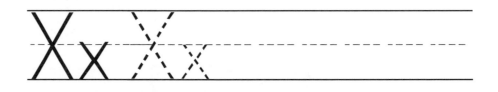

Now color all of the objects below that <u>end</u> with the sound of (x), like ox.

More practice with addition.

5	3	1	2	2	0	4	3
+ 0	+ 2	+ 4	+ 2	+ 3	+ 5	+ 1	+ 1

2	4	3	5	0	3	1	5
+ 3	+ 0	+ 3	+ 1	+ 3	+ 2	+ 1	+ 4

Balloons! Color them the right color.

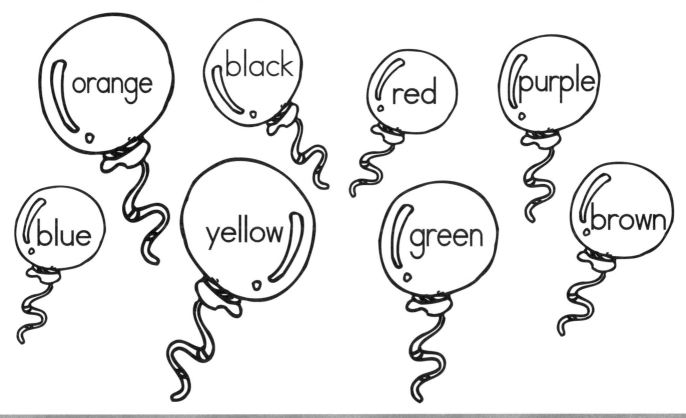

COOKIE JAR PUBLISHING

Yo-yo begins with the sound of (y). Practice writing capital and lowercase (y's).

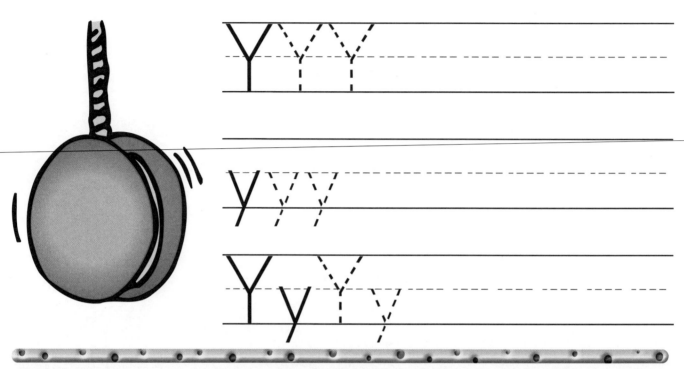

Now color all of the objects below that begin with the sound of (y), like yo-yo.

Addition from 1 to 5.

3 + 1 = _____   4 + 1 = _____   1 + 2 = _____

2 + 2 = _____   1 + 3 = _____   5 + 0 = _____

1 + 4 = _____   2 + 3 = _____   1 + 1 = _____

4 + 0 = _____   2 + 1 = _____   3 + 2 = _____

Can you name these shapes? Color them.

yellow black green blue

purple orange red brown

brown purple yellow black

red blue orange green

Zipper begins with the sound of (z). Practice writing capital and lowercase (z's).

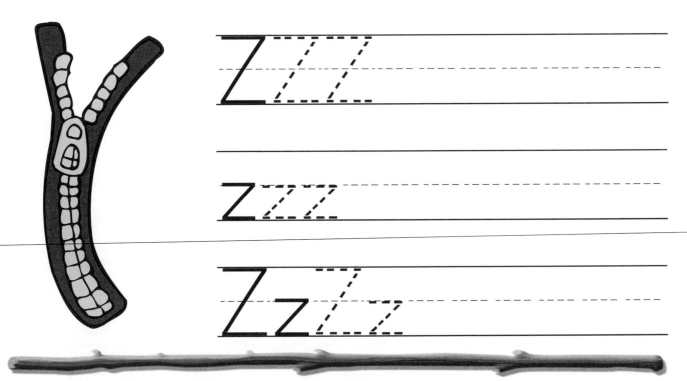

Now color all of the objects below that begin with the sound of (z), like zipper.

Longest or shortest? Largest or smallest?

1. Color the longest fork.

2. Color the shorter rolling pin.

3. Color the largest pie yellow and the smallest pie brown.

Let's try some letters again for added practice! These are all circle letters. Don't let (p) and (b) fool you—the lines go in different directions!

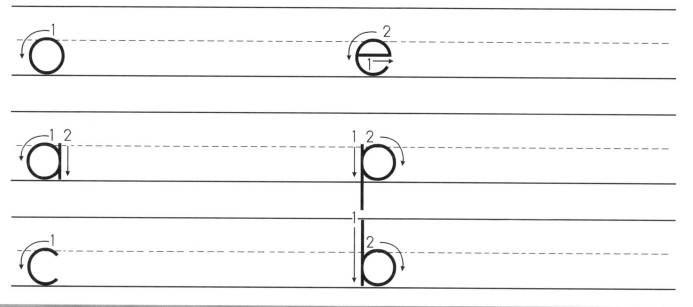

Apple begins with the sound of (a). Practice writing capital and lowercase (a's).

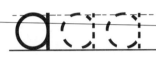

Now color all of the objects below that begin with or have the short (ă) sound, like apple.

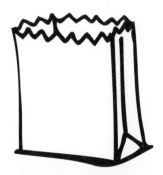

For each problem, put the number of beans in the pot that equal the top number, and take away the number of beans that equal the bottom number. How many beans are left in the pot? Write your answer below the line.

$$\begin{array}{r} 2 \\ -1 \\ \hline \end{array} \qquad \begin{array}{r} 3 \\ -2 \\ \hline \end{array} \qquad \begin{array}{r} 4 \\ -1 \\ \hline \end{array} \qquad \begin{array}{r} 5 \\ -2 \\ \hline \end{array}$$

$$\begin{array}{r} 3 \\ -2 \\ \hline \end{array} \qquad \begin{array}{r} 2 \\ -2 \\ \hline \end{array} \qquad \begin{array}{r} 4 \\ -3 \\ \hline \end{array} \qquad \begin{array}{r} 5 \\ -3 \\ \hline \end{array}$$

Make a rainbow by tracing and coloring the suggested colors.

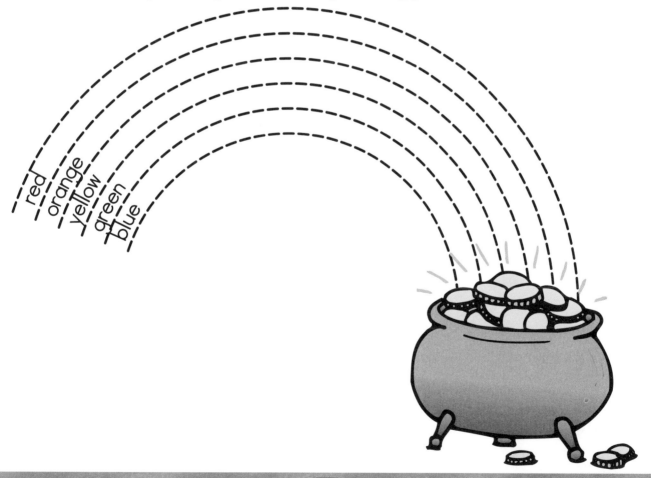

red orange yellow green blue

Say the name of each object and write in the missing short (ă) sound.

EXAMPLE:

 <u>a</u> nt

 f__n

 c__t

 m__p

 v__n

 r__t

We can read words with the short (ă) sound.

m ➭ a ➭ n

Reading the words means putting the sounds together!

man   ant

sad   ran

bag   can

had   tag

Subtraction is easy when you use counters.

$$\begin{array}{r} 2 \\ -\ 1 \\ \hline \end{array}$$ ★ ⊘

$$\begin{array}{r} 4 \\ -\ 2 \\ \hline \end{array}$$ ★ ★ ⊘ ⊘

$$\begin{array}{r} 5 \\ -\ 3 \\ \hline \end{array}$$ ★ ★ ⊘ ⊘ ⊘

$$\begin{array}{r} 5 \\ -\ 2 \\ \hline \end{array}$$

$$\begin{array}{r} 3 \\ -\ 2 \\ \hline \end{array}$$

$$\begin{array}{r} 4 \\ -\ 3 \\ \hline \end{array}$$

$$\begin{array}{r} 2 \\ -\ 2 \\ \hline \end{array}$$

Ice cream cones come in lots of flavors. Color these ice cream cones.

Say the name of each object. Write the letter sounds you hear to spell each word.

EXAMPLE:

rat

___

___

___

___

___

Now sound out and read these short (ă) sentences. Practice reading them fast. "The" is a sight word. Sight words cannot be sounded out.

1. The cat ran and ran.

2. The sad rat sat and sat.

3. Sam has a map. Max has a hat.

4. The fat man has a map.

Subtraction from 1 to 5.

3 – 1 = _____   3 – 2 = _____   4 – 2 = _____

4 – 1 = _____   5 – 4 = _____   5 – 3 = _____

2 – 1 = _____   4 – 3 = _____   4 – 0 = _____

2 – 2 = _____   3 – 3 = _____   5 – 2 = _____

Straight letters are fun to make. Just be sure they stand straight and tall within the lines.

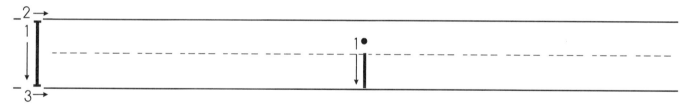

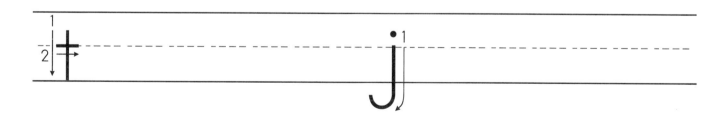

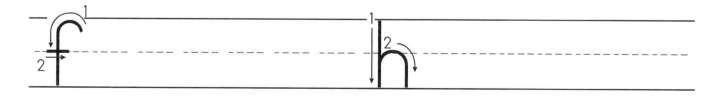

Egg begins with the short (ĕ) sound. Practice writing capital and lowercase (e's).

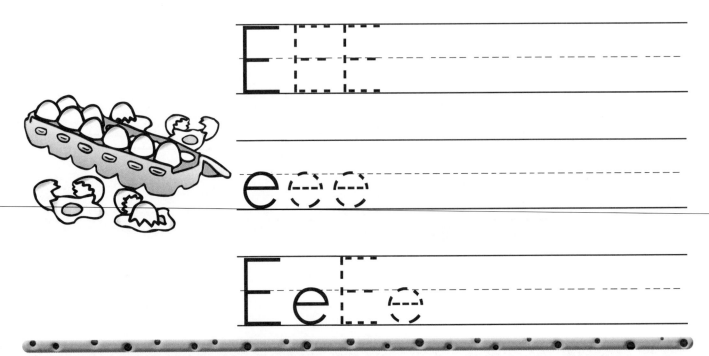

Now color all of the objects below that begin with or have the short (ĕ) sound, like egg.

More practice with subtraction.

5	3	1	4	2	3	5	4
− 1	− 2	− 1	− 2	− 1	− 1	− 5	− 3

3	5	2	4	3	5	4	5
− 3	− 2	− 2	− 1	− 2	− 4	− 4	− 3

Finish the second drawing in each box so it looks just like the first one.

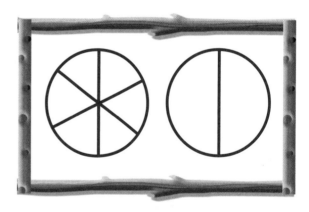
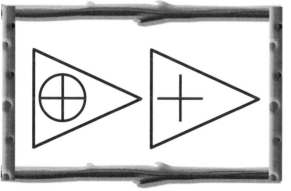
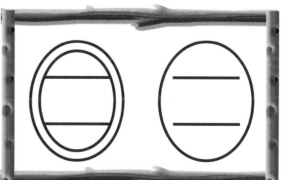

Say the name of each object and write in the missing letter.

EXAMPLE:

b _e_ ll

t __ nt

p __ n

v __ st

__ gg

n __ st

We can read words with the short (ĕ) sound.

pet

ten

den

jet

men

bed

web

hen

Catch these words!

Circle the numbers that are exactly like the number in the first box of each row.

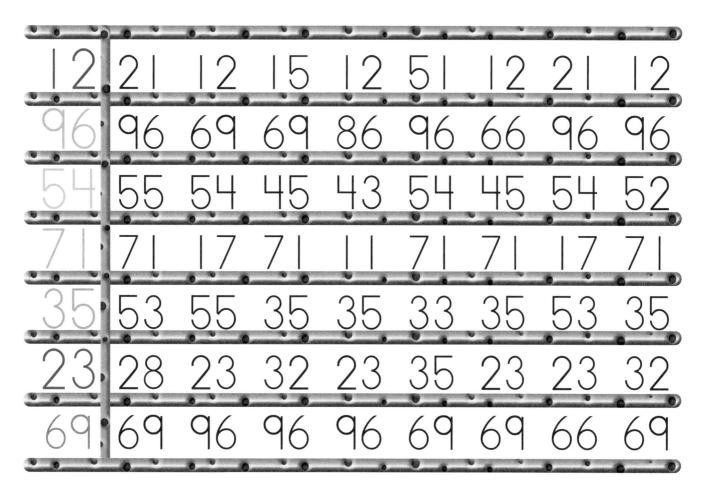

12	21	12	15	12	51	12	21	12
96	96	69	69	86	96	66	96	96
54	55	54	45	43	54	45	54	52
71	71	17	71	11	71	71	17	71
35	53	55	35	35	33	35	53	35
23	28	23	32	23	35	23	23	32
69	69	96	96	96	69	69	66	69

Make your own color chart. Color the crayons the following colors.

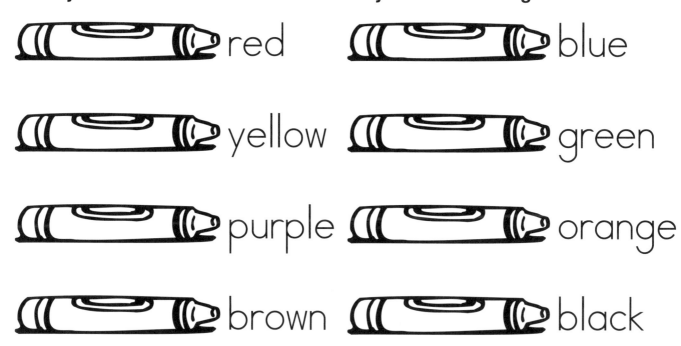

red   blue

yellow   green

purple   orange

brown   black

Say the name of each object. Write the letter sounds you hear to spell each word.

EXAMPLE:

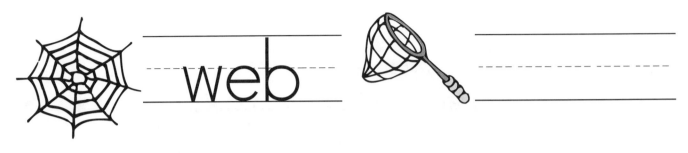

web

_____

_____

_____

_____

Now sound out these short vowel sentences. Practice reading them fast. "The" is a sight word and cannot be sounded out.

1. The T.V. set is off and Jed is in his bed.

2. Peg has the mumps.

3. Ben sends Peg a gift. It is a puppet in a box.

We use a ruler to measure things. This ruler measures inches.

How many inches do you think these lines are?

EXAMPLE:

_____ 4 inches

_____ _____

_____ _____

_____ _____

Practice writing your name on these lines. All three lines are different sizes!

_____

- -

_____

- -

_____

- -

_____

Igloo begins with the short (ĭ) sound. Practice writing capital and lowercase (i's).

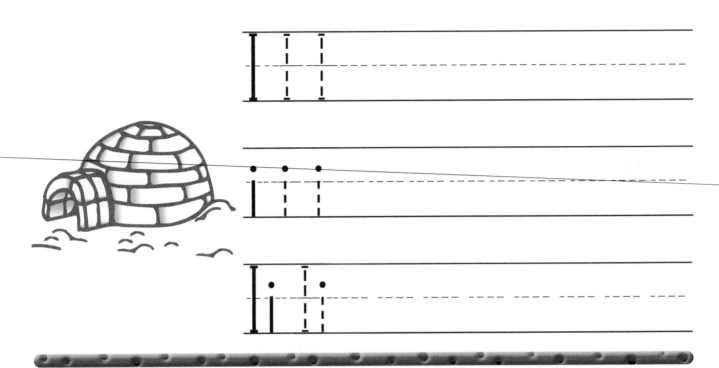

Now color all of the objects below that begin with or have the short (ĭ) sound, like igloo.

Measuring with a ruler is lots of fun. Make your own lines showing the correct inches.

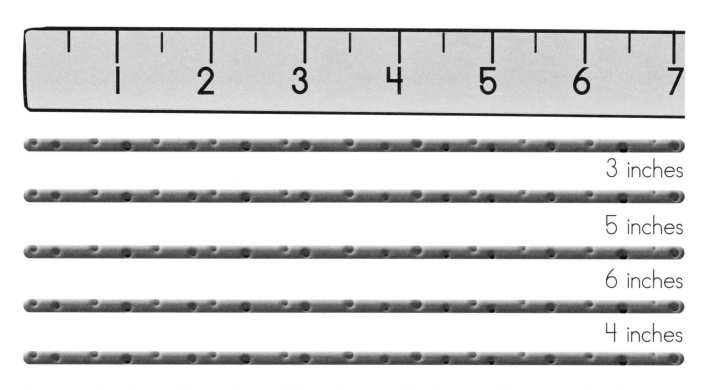

3 inches

5 inches

6 inches

4 inches

Draw and color at least three things in your bedroom. Have an adult help you label them.

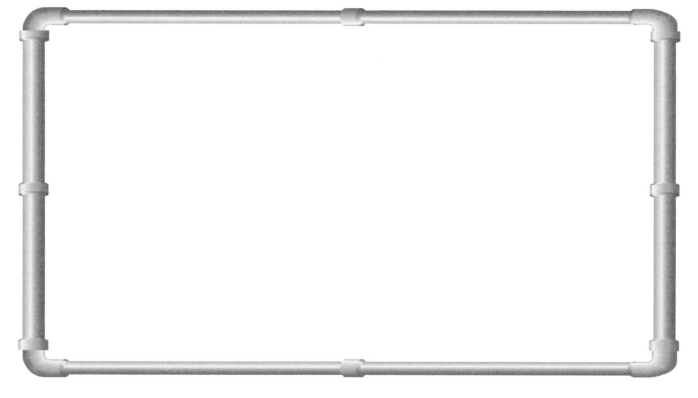

Say the name of each object and write in the missing letter.

EXAMPLE:

 w_i_g

 l__d

 m__lk

 k__ng

 sh__p

 s__x

We can read words with the short (ĭ) sound.

Swimming in a pool of words.

him   hid

did   win

in   it

sit   is

When we count pennies, we count by 1's. If you can, use a real penny to cover each picture as you count. Write the total amount in the blank at the end of each row.

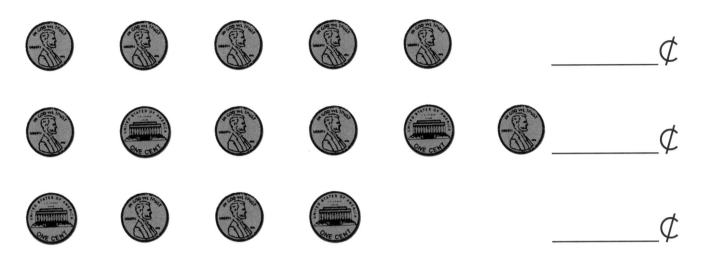

_____¢

_____¢

_____¢

Circle the design that is exactly the same as the design in first box of each row.

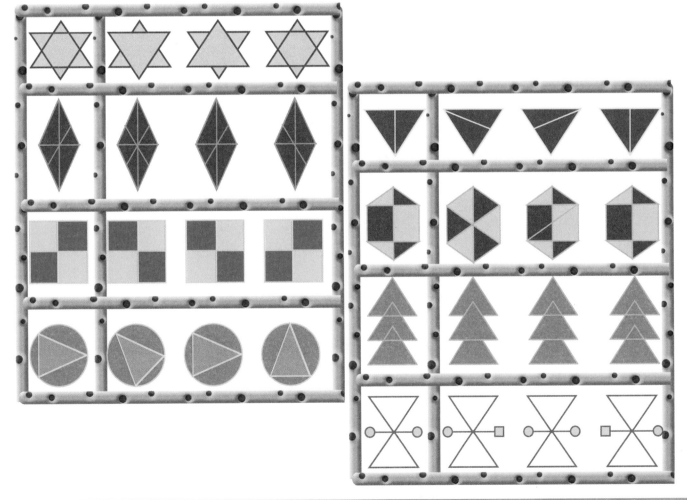

Say the name of each object. Write the letter sounds you hear to spell each word.

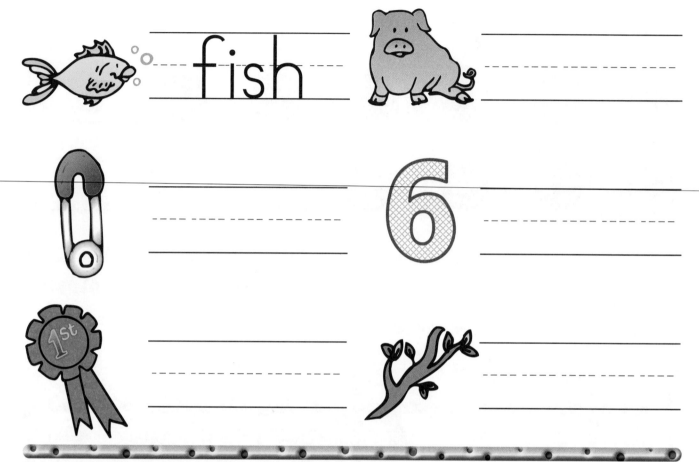

EXAMPLE:

fish

_____

Now sound out and read these short (ĭ) sentences. Practice reading them fast. Remember, "the" is a sight word and cannot be sounded out.

1. Jim hid <u>the</u> lid in a bag.

2. Will <u>the</u> lid fit <u>the</u> tin can?

3. <u>The</u> big fat cat did a flip.

4. Tim will show <u>the</u> big pig to Jill.

5. Kim will sit on <u>the</u> box.

Counting by 5's can be fun when you use your fingers.

EXAMPLE:

5   10   15 _____ _____ _____ _____

_____ _____ _____ _____ _____ _____ _____

Count out loud: 5—10—15—20—25—30—35—40—45—50
                          55—60—65—70—75—80—85—90—95—100

Use a different color crayon to trace the path from shape to matching shape.

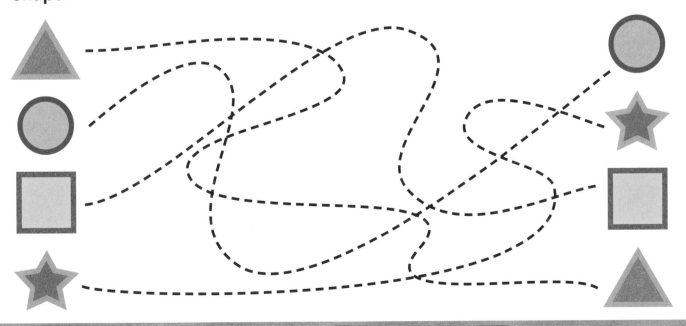

COOKIE JAR PUBLISHING

Octopus begins with the short (ŏ) sound. Practice writing capital and lowercase (o's).

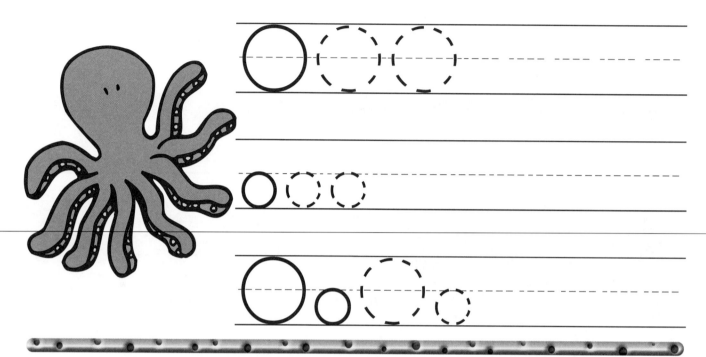

Now color all of the objects below that begin with or have the short (ŏ) sound, like octopus.

When we count nickels, we count by 5's. If you can, use a real nickel to cover each picture as you count. Write the total amount in the blank at the end of each row.

_____¢

_____¢

_____¢

Crossword puzzle: Fill in the squares with the picture word.

EXAMPLE:

Say the name of each object and write in the missing letter.

EXAMPLE:

 d_o_ll

 f__x

 l__ck

 sh__p

 m__p

 r__ck

We can read words with the short (ŏ) sound.

These words won't "out fox" you!

dog   top

hot   fog

box   got

pop   rob

Practice writing to 100 by 10's.

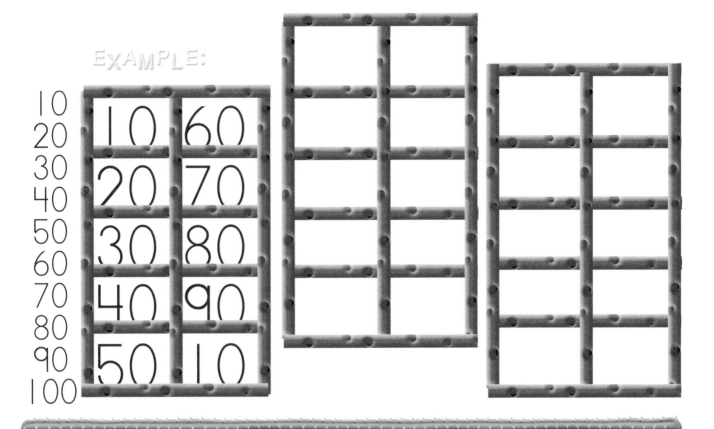

EXAMPLE:

10	60
20	70
30	80
40	90
50	10

10
20
30
40
50
60
70
80
90
100

Word search: Find the words and circle them.

 sun    men

 pin    sad

 hen    up

w	p	i	n	u
s	a	d	c	o
l	f	s	u	n
h	e	n	p	m
t	m	e	n	b

Say the name of each object. Write down the letter sounds you hear to spell the word.

EXAMPLE:

fan

Now sound out these short vowel sentences. Practice reading the sentences fast. Remember, "the" is a sight word and cannot be sounded out.

1. The frog can jump on top of the box.
2. The fox, dog, and rat ran in the hot sun.
3. The hog sat on a rock.
4. Bob sat in the fog all day long.

When we count dimes, we count by 10's. If you can, cover each picture with a real dime as you count. Write the total amount in the blank at the end of each row.

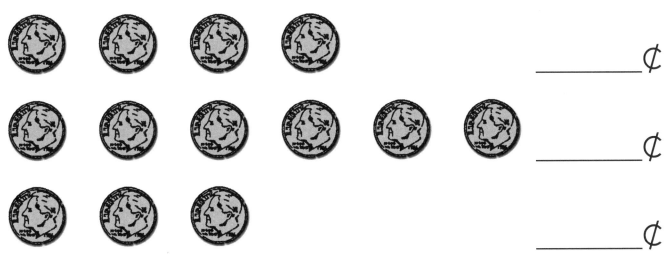

_____¢

_____¢

_____¢

Make shapes exactly like the first one in each row. The dots will help you.

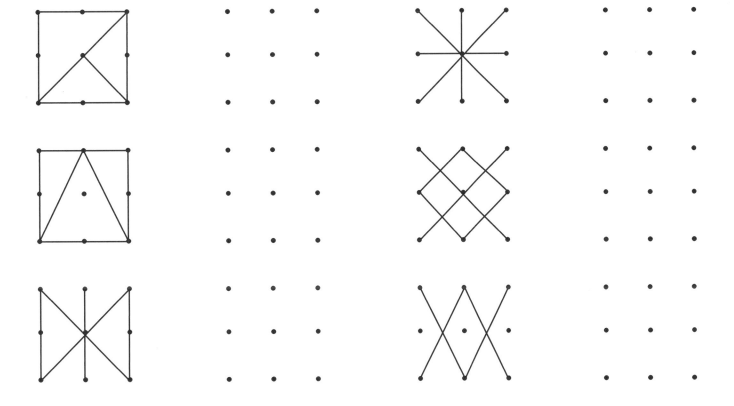

Umbrella begins with the short (ŭ) sound. Practice writing capital and lowercase (u's).

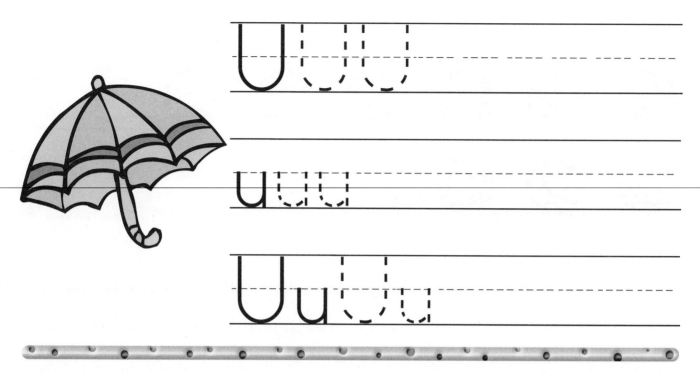

Now color all of the objects below that begin with or have the short (ŭ) sound, like umbrella.

Summer Activities

Grade K-1

Three-in-a-Row

Make your own tic-tac-toe game. Collect several smooth, flat stones. On half of the stones paint an "X." On the other half paint an "O." Be sure that you have 5 of each.

Use chalk to draw a big **#** on the sidewalk or other flat piece of cement. Now have a competition with your friends. When you are done, store your stones in an old coffee can or bucket.

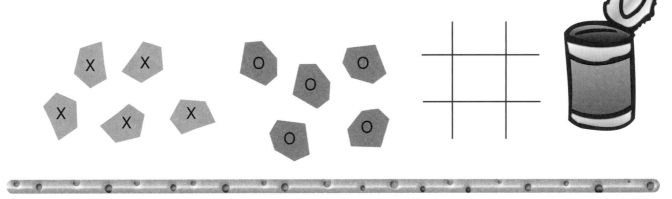

Family Mural

Paint a mural of your family history on butcher paper. All family members should participate and paint a portion of the mural.

It can be a historical moment, or a collection of pictures that represents accomplishments of your family members.

Try Something New
Fun Activity Ideas

 1 Play hopscotch, marbles, or jump rope.

 2 Visit a fire station.

 3 Make a map of you neighborhood.

 4 Make up a song.

 5 Make a hut out of blankets and chairs.

 6 Put a note in a helium balloon and let it go.

 7 Start a journal. Write about your favorite vacation memories.

 8 Make 3-D nature art. Glue leaves, twigs, dirt, grass, and rocks on paper.

 9 Find an ant colony. Spill some food and see what happens.

 10 Play charades.

 11 Make up a story by drawing pictures.

 12 Do something to help the environment. Clean up an area near your house.

 13 Weed a row in the garden. Mom will love it!

 14 Take a trip to a park.

 15 Learn about different road signs.

Count the money in these hands and write the correct amount.

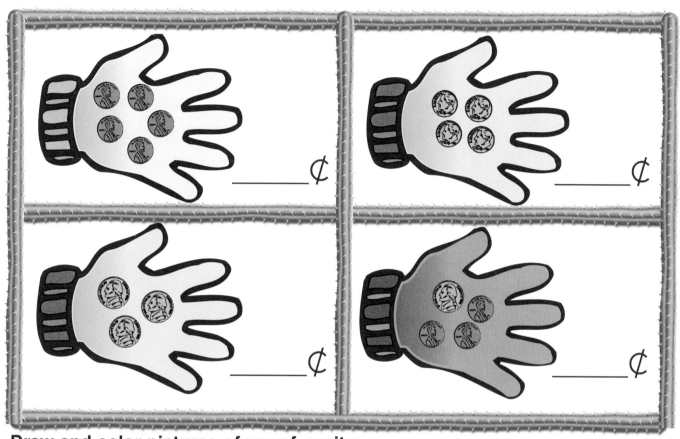

_____¢   _____¢

_____¢   _____¢

Draw and color pictures of your favorite:

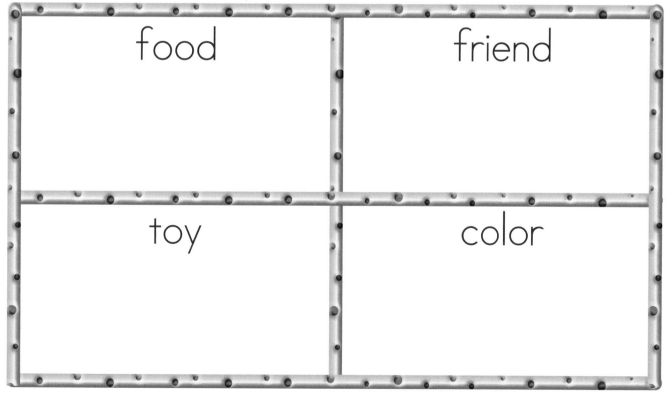

food   friend

toy   color

Say the name of each object and write in the missing letter.

EXAMPLE:

 b_u_g

 pl__g

 d___ck

 br___sh

 t___b

 m___g

We can read words with the short (ŭ) sound.

mud	fun
dug	mug
cut	us
up	hut

You're not all wet when you work on these words!

Count the wheels on the train by 2's.

Complete this crossword puzzle.

EXAMPLE:

Across:

4.

5.

Down:

1.

3.

2. 6

6.

Say the name of each object. Write the letter sounds you hear to spell each word.

EXAMPLE:

sun

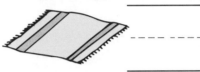

Sound out these short vowel sentences. Practice reading them fast. "The" is a sight word and cannot be sounded out.

1. Can a bug hum in a jug?

2. It is fun in <u>the</u> tub.

3. <u>The</u> man can hug <u>the</u> pup.

4. Ann has mud in <u>the</u> mug, yuck.

Addition to 10.

6 + 2 = ___   5 + 1 = ___   4 + 3 = ___

1 + 7 = ___   2 + 8 = ___   9 + 0 = ___

3 + 5 = ___   4 + 6 = ___   7 + 2 = ___

8 + 1 = ___   1 + 9 = ___   6 + 3 = ___

5 + 4 = ___   6 + 1 = ___   3 + 7 = ___

0 + 8 = ___   3 + 4 = ___   2 + 5 = ___

Search for the number words from 1 to 10.

1. one
2. two
3. three
4. four
5. five
6. six
7. seven
8. eight
9. nine
10. ten

m	a	z	t	s	i	x
t	e	n	w	x	o	p
y	i	f	o	u	r	o
f	g	s	e	v	e	n
i	h	l	n	i	n	e
v	t	h	r	e	e	b
e	c	d	e	f	g	h

**Find the objects with the beginning sound of the letter in each box.
Color them.**

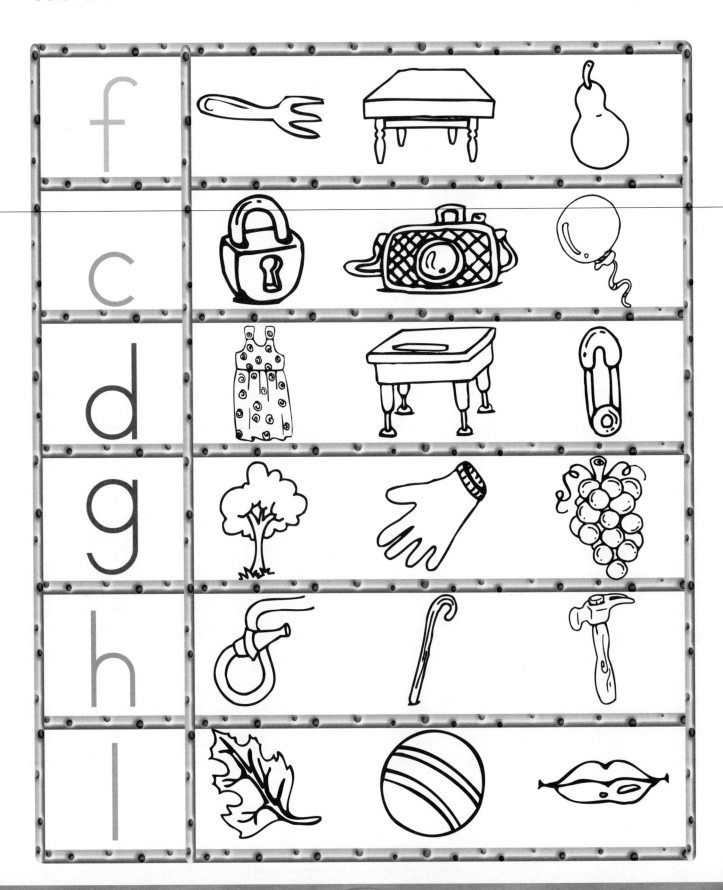

Addition to 10.

$$5 \quad 4 \quad 9 \quad 2 \quad 3 \quad 8 \quad 6$$
$$\underline{+3} \quad \underline{+5} \quad \underline{+1} \quad \underline{+7} \quad \underline{+4} \quad \underline{+2} \quad \underline{+3}$$

$$9 \quad 1 \quad 4 \quad 5 \quad 6 \quad 3 \quad 2$$
$$\underline{+0} \quad \underline{+8} \quad \underline{+5} \quad \underline{+2} \quad \underline{+2} \quad \underline{+5} \quad \underline{+4}$$

Trace the first design, then make one exactly like it.

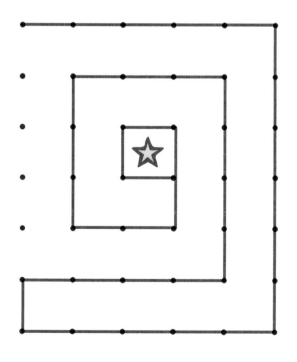

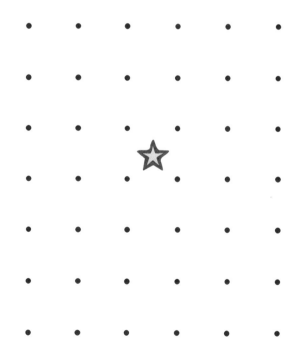

COOKIE JAR PUBLISHING

**Find the objects with the beginning sound of the letter in each box.
Color them.**

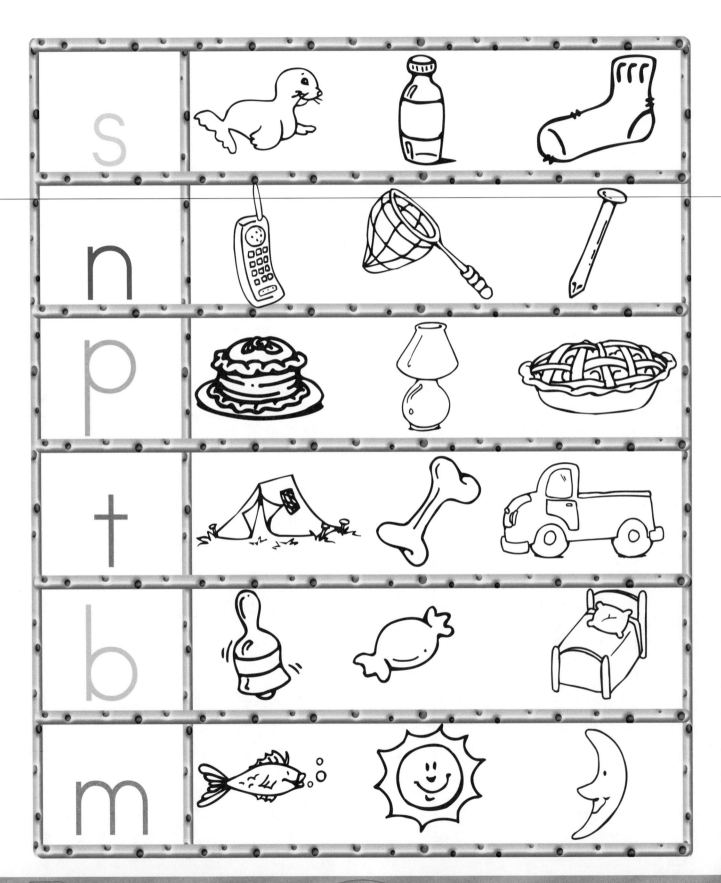

Touch each number and say it out loud with an adult in your family.

0	1	2	3	4	5	6	7	8	9	10	11
12	13	14	15	16	17	18	19	20	21	22	23
24	25	26	27	28	29	30	31	32	33	34	35
36	37	38	39	40	41	42	43	44	45	46	47
48	49	50	51	52	53	54	55	56	57	58	59
60	61	62	63	64	65	66	67	68	69	70	71
72	73	74	75	76	77	78	79	80	81	82	83
84	85	86	87	88	89	90	91	92	93	94	95
96	97	98	99	100							

Color the object red in each box you think would make the most noise.
Color the object green in each box you think would make the least noise.

1.

2.

3.

4.

**Find the objects with the beginning sound of the letter in each box.
Color them.**

Write the numbers 1 to 50 in the empty boxes.

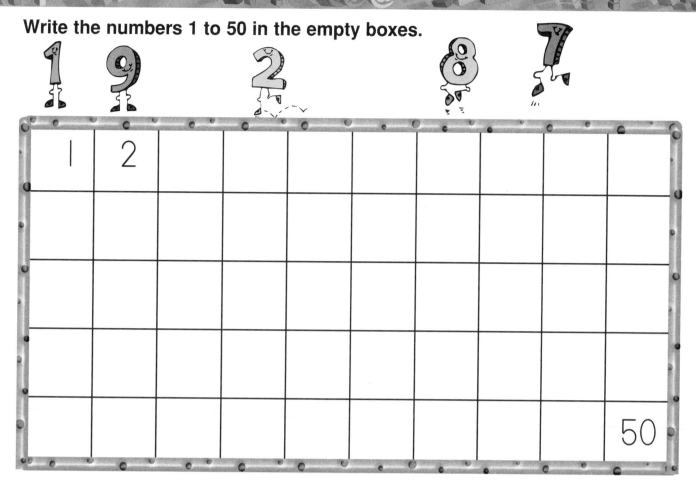

1	2								
									50

Read the word in each row and color the two pictures that rhyme with it.

cat

fan

top

Say the picture word. Write the beginning letter sound you hear.

EXAMPLE:

b

Subtraction to 10.

5 – 2 = ___	9 – 3 = ___	10 – 1 = ___
7 – 4 = ___	6 – 2 = ___	8 – 5 = ___
9 – 5 = ___	10 – 2 = ___	7 – 3 = ___
8 – 4 = ___	5 – 5 = ___	6 – 3 = ___
10 – 0 = ___	6 – 4 = ___	5 – 3 = ___
9 – 4 = ___	8 – 7 = ___	7 – 2 = ___

Match the rhyming pictures.

EXAMPLE:

COOKIE JAR PUBLISHING

Say the picture word. Write the beginning letter sound you hear.

EXAMPLE:

m

_____

_____

_____

_____

_____

_____

_____

_____

_____

_____

_____

_____

Subtraction to 10.

7	8	9	6	5	8	9
− 3	− 5	− 1	− 2	− 4	− 3	− 5

6	8	5	7	9	8	9
− 3	− 7	− 2	− 5	− 4	− 6	− 3

Draw and color something real.	Draw and color something make-believe.

Say the picture word. Circle the ending letter sound you hear.

EXAMPLE:		5	
w b (t)	p s g	z v p	k n m
g c d	j k w	r z l	d p c
k f x	t l n	h r b	f t l
c d k	h j g	n m h	t j h
r h n	t m c	j r s	b p d

Write numbers 26 to 75 in the empty boxes.

26	27								
									75

Trace the first design, then make one exactly like it.

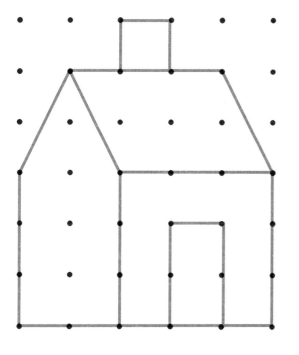

Say the picture word. Write the ending letter sound you hear.

EXAMPLE:

 g

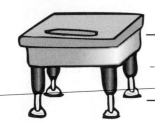

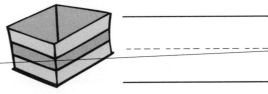

Addition and subtraction. Watch the signs carefully.

$$
\begin{array}{ccccccc}
7 & 8 & 9 & 6 & 5 & 1 & 2 \\
+3 & -2 & -5 & +2 & +3 & +8 & +5
\end{array}
$$

$$
\begin{array}{ccccccc}
6 & 8 & 9 & 7 & 9 & 8 & 5 \\
-3 & -7 & +1 & -5 & -4 & -6 & +4
\end{array}
$$

Circle the two objects in each row that rhyme. Color the object that <u>does not</u> rhyme.

Say the name of each object. Write the beginning and ending letter sounds you hear.

d ___ k

Addition and subtraction. Watch the signs carefully.

9 – 3 = ____   6 + 4 = ____   5 + 3 = ____

2 + 7 = ____   8 – 2 = ____   7 – 5 = ____

4 + 5 = ____   6 – 3 = ____   6 + 3 = ____

8 – 3 = ____   9 – 4 = ____   7 – 3 = ____

5 + 4 = ____   8 – 6 = ____   9 – 5 = ____

6 + 2 = ____   4 – 3 = ____   7 + 2 = ____

Say the name of the picture in each box, then draw something that rhymes with it.

COOKIE JAR PUBLISHING

Practice sounding out and reading these long (ā) words.

bake   cane   cage   tape
skate   lane   page   cape

apron   gate   snail   chain
ape   ate   pail   train

Say the name of each picture. Write down the letter sounds you hear to spell the word.

_ _ _ _ e   _ _ _ _ e   _ _ _ _ _ _ e

_ _ _ i _   _ _ _ i _   _ _ _ i _

Sound out these long vowel sentences. Practice reading them fast. "The" is a sight word and cannot be sounded out.

1. I can make a big cake.

2. The fat snail is in a red pail.

3. Gail can skate with her cape.

Write the numbers 51 to 100 in the empty boxes.

51	52								
									100

Draw and color pictures of the members of your family. Can you write their names by their pictures?

Practice sounding out and reading these long (ē) words.

| eel | tree | feet | freeze |
| feel | seed | sweet | breeze |

| peas | beads | beak | beach |
| meal | beans | jeans | steam |

Say the name of each picture. Spell it out with the letter sounds you hear.

3

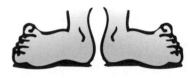

__ __ __ __   __ __ __ __   __ __ __ __

__ __ a __ __   __ __ a __   __ __ a __

Sound out these long vowel sentences. Practice reading them fast.
"The" is a sight word and cannot be sounded out.

1. The big tree has lots of green leaves.

2. Take a nap, Jean, and go to sleep.

3. The queen has a string of beads.

What about adding or subtracting with doubles?

$$1 \quad 2 \quad 3 \quad 4 \quad 5 \quad 6 \quad 0$$
$$+1 \quad +2 \quad +3 \quad +4 \quad +5 \quad +6 \quad +0$$

$$1 \quad 2 \quad 3 \quad 4 \quad 5 \quad 6 \quad 0$$
$$-1 \quad -2 \quad -3 \quad -4 \quad -5 \quad -6 \quad -0$$

Finish drawing the other half of the pictures, then color.

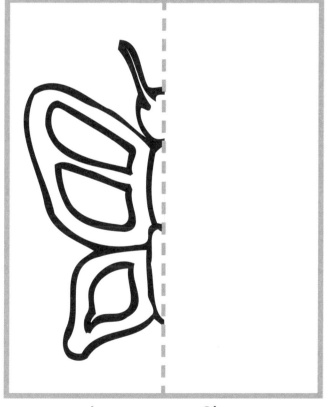

butterfly

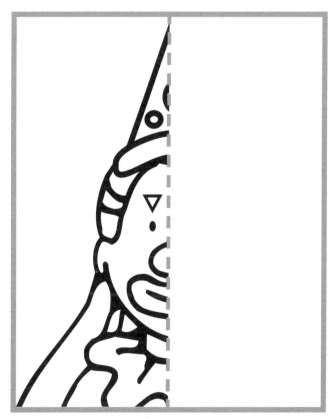

clown

COOKIE JAR PUBLISHING

Practice sounding out and reading these long (ī) words.

pie	wide	ripe	like
tie	side	pipe	hike

life	hire	rise	mile
wife	tire	wise	file

Say the name of each picture and write in the letter sounds you hear to spell the word.

_ _ _ e   _ _ _ e   _ _ _ _ e

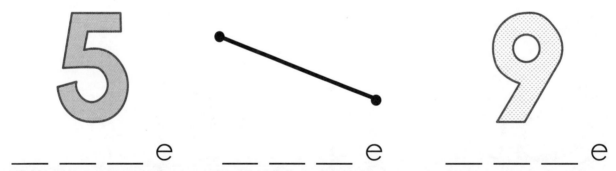

_ _ _ e   _ _ _ e   _ _ _ _ e

Sound out and read these sentences. Practice reading them fast.

1. The bike is Tim's size to ride.
2. I can swim and run a mile.
3. Jill likes to swim and dive.
4. The sun will shine and I will fly my five kites.

Circle the number in each box that is more.

EXAMPLE:

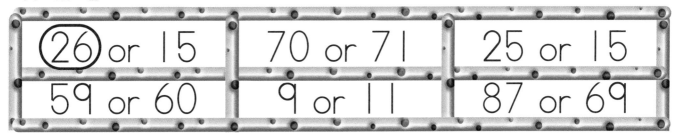

(26) or 15	70 or 71	25 or 15
59 or 60	9 or 11	87 or 69

Circle the number in each box that is less.

EXAMPLE:

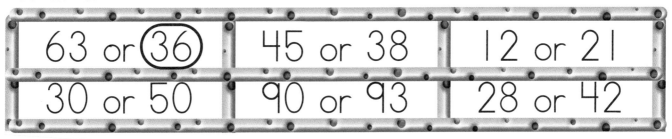

63 or (36)	45 or 38	12 or 21
30 or 50	90 or 93	28 or 42

Using the letters in the box, see how many words you can make with these word endings.

r s t c b m p n

EXAMPLE:

_p_ an	___at	___in
___an	___at	___in
___an	___at	___ug
___an	___at	___ug
___ut	___et	___op
___ut	___et	___op

Practice sounding out and reading these long (ō) words.

| hose | note | joke | bone |
| rose | quote | poke | cone |

| toad | boat | roast | goat |
| float | toast | soap | soak |

Say the name of each picture. Write down the letter sounds you hear to spell the word.

__ __ a __   __ __ a __   __ __ a __ __

__ __ __ __ e   __ __ __ e   __ __ __ e

Sound out and read these sentences. Practice reading them fast.

1. The roast is on top of the stove.
2. The dog stole his bone from the store.
3. Joe drove the dog back to the store.
4. Joan wore a rose on her torn dress.

Write in the missing numbers from 1 to 100.

0	1	2	_	4	5	_	_	_	9	10	11
12	13	_	_	16	_	_	_	20	21	_	_
24	_	26	_	_	29	_	31	_	_	34	_
36	_	_	_	40	_	_	_	45	46	_	
_	_	_	51	_	_	54	_	_	57	58	_
60	_	_	_	64	_	66	_	_	69	_	71
_	73	_	_	76	77	_	_	_	81	82	83
					89						
_	_	_	_	_	_	_	_	_	_	_	_
_	_	_	_	100							

Make your own design by connecting the dots.

Practice sounding out and reading these long (ū) words.

cute	mule	fume	tube
cube	mute	fuse	rude

bugle	blue	true	prune
flute	clue	glue	tune

Say the name of each picture. Write down the letter sounds you hear to spell the word.

__ __ __ e

__ __ __ e

__ __ __ e

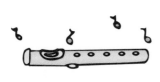

__ __ __ __ e

__ __ __ e   __ __ __ __ e

Sound out and read these sentences. Practice reading them fast.

1. The bad dude broke the rule.
2. Cute June likes to play music on the flute.
3. The mule ate blue prunes.
4. It is true, I can rescue the unicorn.

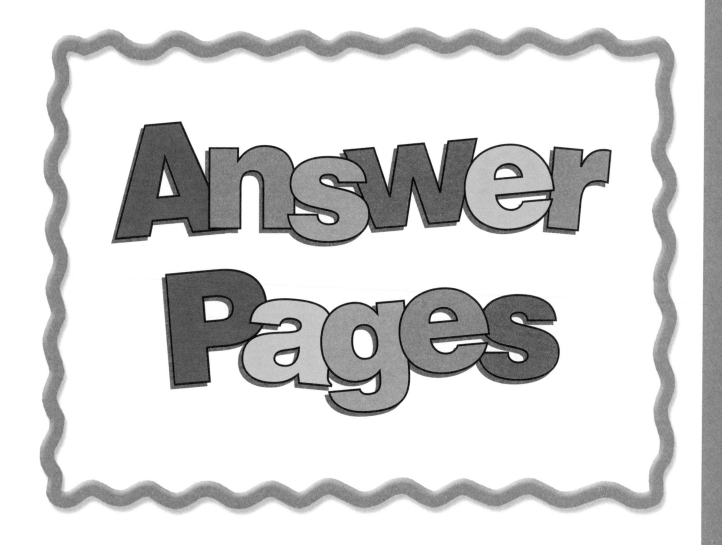

Page 3

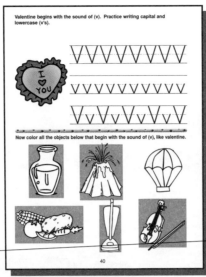

Page 4

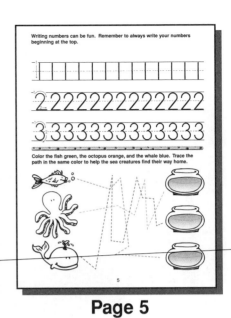

Page 5

Page 6

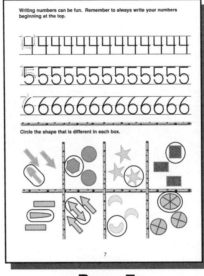

Page 7

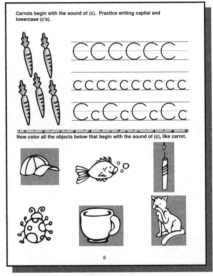

Page 8

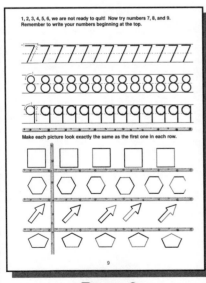

Page 9

Page 10

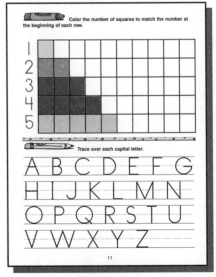

Page 11

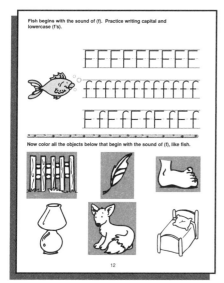

Page 12

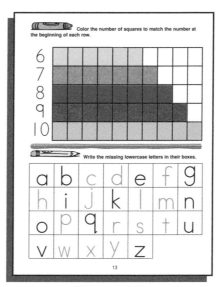

Page 13

Page 14

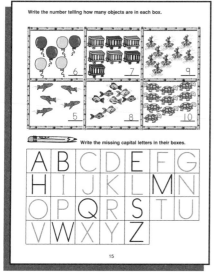

Page 15

Page 16

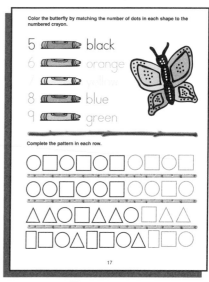

Page 17

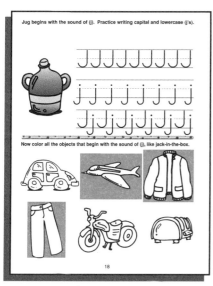

Page 18

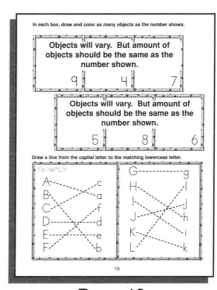

Page 19

Page 20

Page 21

Page 22

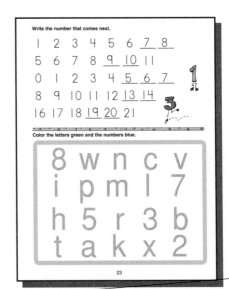

Page 23

Page 24

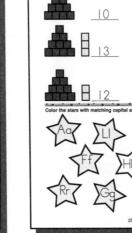

Page 25

Page 26

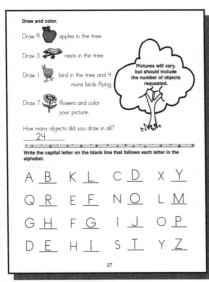

Page 27

Page 28

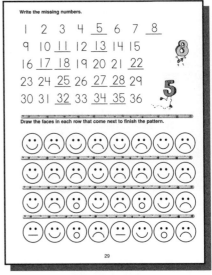

Page 29

Page 30

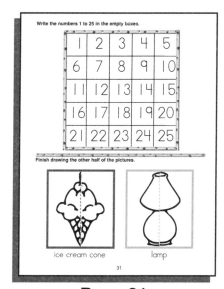

Page 31

Page 32

Page 35

Page 36

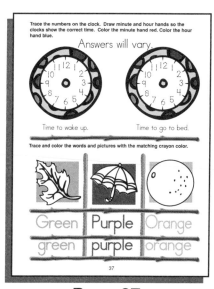

Page 37

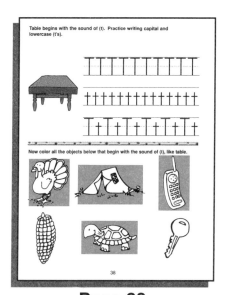

Page 38

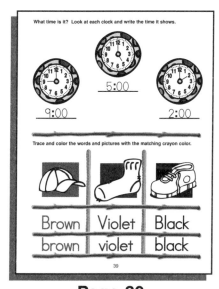

Page 39

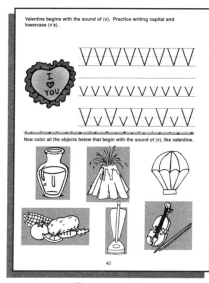

Page 40

Page 41

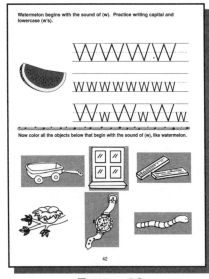

Page 42

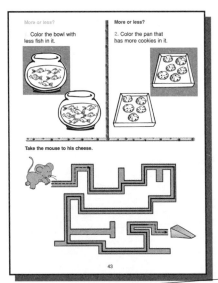

Page 43

Page 44

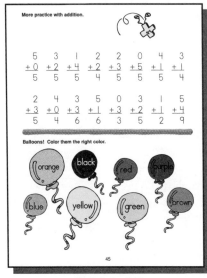

Page 45

Page 46

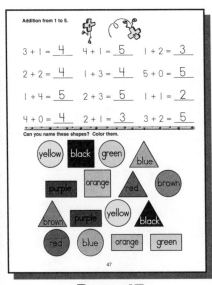

Page 47

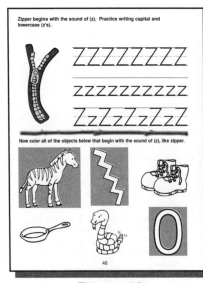

Page 48

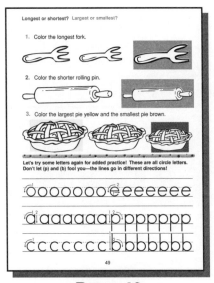

Page 49

Page 50

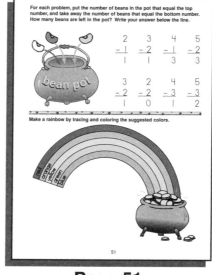

Page 51

Page 52

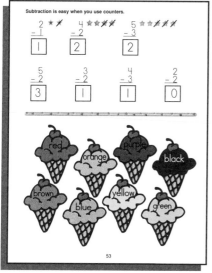

Page 53

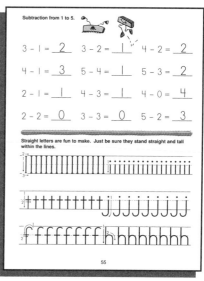

Page 54

Page 55

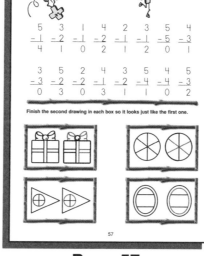

Page 56

Page 57

Page 58

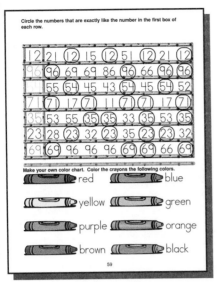

Page 59

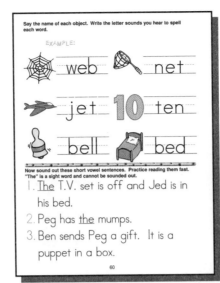

Page 60

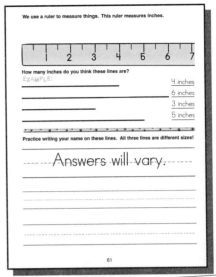

Page 61

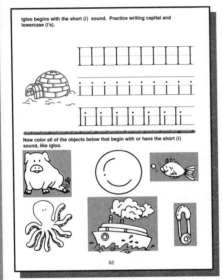

Page 62

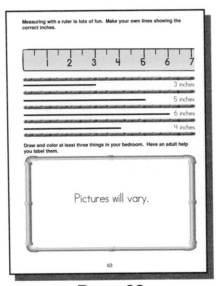

Page 63

Page 64

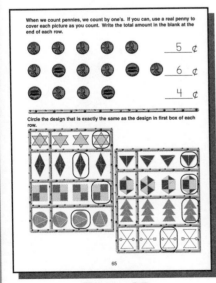

Page 65

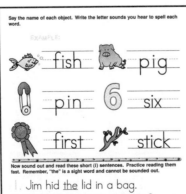

Page 66

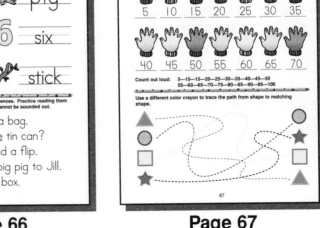

Page 67

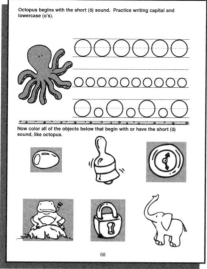

Page 68

Page 69

Page 70

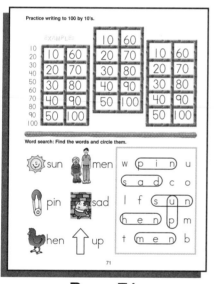

Page 71

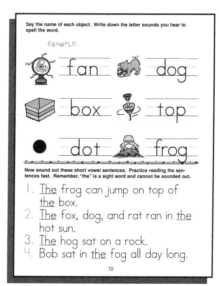

Page 72

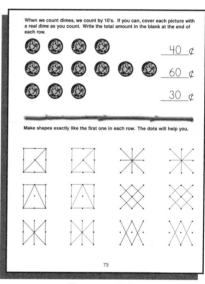

Page 73

Page 74

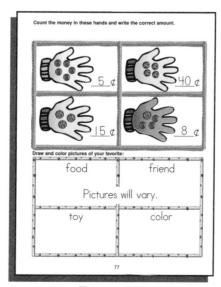

Page 77

Page 78

Page 79

Count the wheels on the train by 2's.

2 4 6 8
16 14 12 10
18 20

Complete this crossword puzzle.

EXAMPLE:

b u s
f o x
i m v
s i x
m a a
p e n

Across:
4.
5.

Down:
1.
3.
2. 6
6.

79

Page 80

Say the name of each object. Write the letter sounds you hear to spell each word.

sun   gum
bus   rug
cup   nut

Sound out these short vowel sentences. Practice reading them fast. "The" is a sight word and cannot be sounded out.

1. Can a bug hum in a jug?

It is fun in the tub.

3. The man can hug the pup.

Ann has mud in the mug, yuck.

80

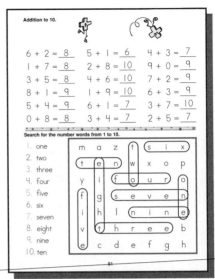

Page 81

Addition to 10.

6 + 2 = 8   5 + 1 = 6   4 + 3 = 7
1 + 7 = 8   2 + 8 = 10   9 + 0 = 9
3 + 5 = 8   4 + 6 = 10   7 + 2 = 9
8 + 1 = 9   1 + 9 = 10   6 + 3 = 9
5 + 4 = 9   6 + 1 = 7   3 + 7 = 10
0 + 8 = 8   3 + 4 = 7   2 + 5 = 7

Search for the number words from 1 to 10.

1. one
2. two
3. three
4. four
5. five
6. six
7. seven
8. eight
9. nine
10. ten

m a z t s i x
t e n w x o p
y i f o u r o
f g h s e v e n
i l n i n e e
h t h r e e b
e c d e f g h

81

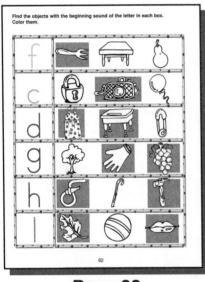

Page 82

Find the objects with the beginning sound of the letter in each box. Color them.

f
c
d
g
h
l

82

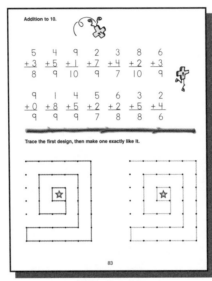

Page 83

Addition to 10.

5   4   9   2   3   8   6
+3   +5   +1   +7   +4   +2   +3
8   9   10   9   7   10   9

9   1   4   5   6   3   2
+0   +8   +5   +2   +2   +5   +4
9   9   9   7   8   8   6

Trace the first design, then make one exactly like it.

83

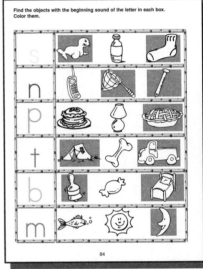

Page 84

Find the objects with the beginning sound of the letter in each box. Color them.

s
n
p
t
b
m

84

Page 85

Touch each number and say it out loud with an adult in your family.

0 1 2 3 4 5 6 7 8 9 10 11
12 13 14 15 16 17 18 19 20 21 22 23
24 25 26 27 28 29 30 31 32 33 34 35
36 37 38 39 40 41 42 43 44 45 46 47
48 49 50 51 52 53 54 55 56 57 58 59
60 61 62 63 64 65 66 67 68 69 70 71
72 73 74 75 76 77 78 79 80 81 82 83
84 85 86 87 88 89 90 91 92 93 94 95
96 97 98 99 100

Color the object red in each box you think would make the most noise.
Color the object green in each box you think would make the least noise.

1.   2.
Answers will vary.
3.   4.

85

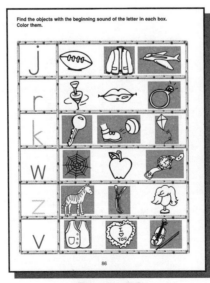

Page 86

Find the objects with the beginning sound of the letter in each box. Color them.

j
r
k
w
z
v

86

Page 87

Write the numbers 1 to 50 in the empty boxes.

1 2 3 4 5 6 7 8 9 10
11 12 13 14 15 16 17 18 19 20
21 22 23 24 25 26 27 28 29 30
31 32 33 34 35 36 37 38 39 40
41 42 43 44 45 46 47 48 49 50

Read the word in each row and color the two pictures that rhyme with it.

cat
fan
top

87

Page 88

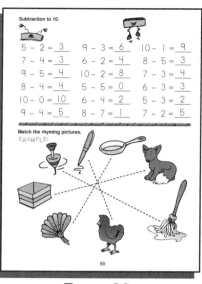

Page 89

Page 90

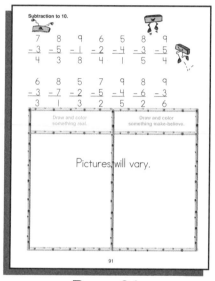

Page 91

Page 92

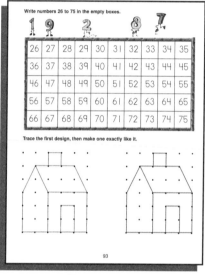

Page 93

Page 94

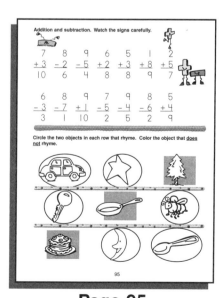

Page 95

Page 96

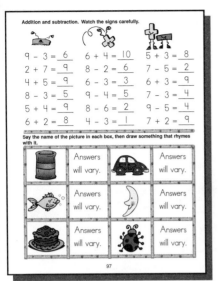

Page 97

Addition and subtraction. Watch the signs carefully.

9 − 3 = 6   6 + 4 = 10   5 + 3 = 8
2 + 7 = 9   8 − 2 = 6   7 − 5 = 2
4 + 5 = 9   6 − 3 = 3   6 + 3 = 9
8 − 3 = 5   9 − 4 = 5   7 − 3 = 4
5 + 4 = 9   8 − 6 = 2   9 − 5 = 4
6 + 2 = 8   4 − 3 = 1   7 + 2 = 9

Say the name of the picture in each box, then draw something that rhymes with it.

	Answers will vary.		Answers will vary.
	Answers will vary.		Answers will vary.
	Answers will vary.		Answers will vary.

97

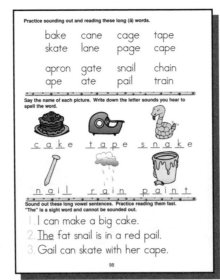

Page 98

Practice sounding out and reading these long (ā) words.

bake   cane   cage   tape
skate   lane   page   cape

apron   gate   snail   chain
ape   ate   pail   train

Say the name of each picture. Write down the letter sounds you hear to spell the word.

c a k e   t a p e   s n a k e

n a i l   r a i n   p a i n t

Sound out these long vowel sentences. Practice reading them fast. "The" is a sight word and cannot be sounded out.

1. I can make a big cake.
2. The fat snail is in a red pail.
3. Gail can skate with her cape.

98

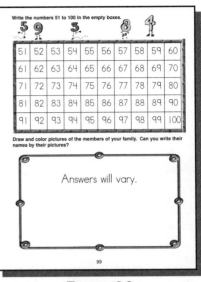

Page 99

Write the numbers 51 to 100 in the empty boxes.

51	52	53	54	55	56	57	58	59	60
61	62	63	64	65	66	67	68	69	70
71	72	73	74	75	76	77	78	79	80
81	82	83	84	85	86	87	88	89	90
91	92	93	94	95	96	97	98	99	100

Draw and color pictures of the members of your family. Can you write their names by their pictures?

Answers will vary.

99

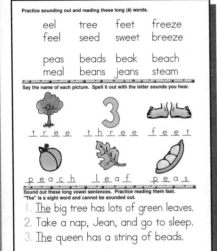

Page 100

Practice sounding out and reading these long (ē) words.

eel   tree   feet   freeze
feel   seed   sweet   breeze

peas   beads   beak   beach
meal   beans   jeans   steam

Say the name of each picture. Spell it out with the letter sounds you hear.

t r e e   t h r e e   f e e t

p e a c h   l e a f   p e a s

Sound out these long vowel sentences. Practice reading them fast. "The" is a sight word and cannot be sounded out.

1. The big tree has lots of green leaves.
2. Take a nap, Jean, and go to sleep.
3. The queen has a string of beads.

100

Page 101

What about adding or subtracting with doubles?

1	2	3	4	5	6	0
+1	+2	+3	+4	+5	+6	+0
2	4	6	8	10	12	0

1	2	3	4	5	6	0
−1	−2	−3	−4	−5	−6	−0
0	0	0	0	0	0	0

Finish drawing the other half of the pictures, then color.

butterfly   clown

101

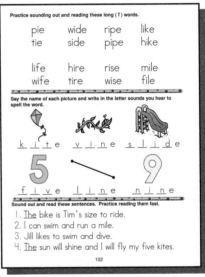

Page 102

Practice sounding out and reading these long (ī) words.

pie   wide   ripe   like
tie   side   pipe   hike

life   hire   rise   mile
wife   tire   wise   file

Say the name of each picture and write in the letter sounds you hear to spell the word.

k i t e   v i n e   s l i d e

f i v e   l i n e   n i n e

Sound out and read these sentences. Practice reading them fast.

1. The bike is Tim's size to ride.
2. I can swim and run a mile.
3. Jill likes to swim and dive.
4. The sun will shine and I will fly my five kites.

102

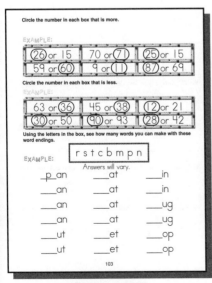

Page 103

Circle the number in each box that is more.

EXAMPLE:

| 26 or 15 | 70 or 71 | 25 or 15 |
| 59 or 60 | 9 or 11 | 87 or 69 |

Circle the number in each box that is less.

EXAMPLE:

| 63 or 36 | 45 or 38 | 12 or 21 |
| 30 or 50 | 90 or 93 | 28 or 42 |

Using the letters in the box, see how many words you can make with these word endings.

| r s t c b m p n |

EXAMPLE: Answers will vary.

p an   ___at   ___in
___an   ___at   ___in
___an   ___at   ___ug
___an   ___at   ___ug
___ut   ___et   ___op
___ut   ___et   ___op

103

Page 104

Practice sounding out and reading these long (ō) words.

hose   note   joke   bone
rose   quote   poke   cone

toad   boat   roast   goat
float   toast   soap   soak

Say the name of each picture. Write down the letter sounds you hear to spell the word.

b o a t   g o a t   t o a s t

s t o v e   n o t e   r o s e

Sound out and read these sentences. Practice reading them fast.

1. The roast is on top of the stove.
2. The dog stole his bone from the store.
3. Joe drove the dog back to the store.
4. Joan wore a rose on her torn dress.

104

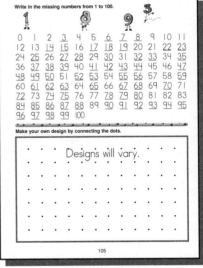

Page 105

Write in the missing numbers from 1 to 100.

0 1 2 3 4 5 6 7 8 9 10 11
12 13 14 15 16 17 18 19 20 21 22 23
24 25 26 27 28 29 30 31 32 33 34 35
36 37 38 39 40 41 42 43 44 45 46 47
48 49 50 51 52 53 54 55 56 57 58 59
60 61 62 63 64 65 66 67 68 69 70 71
72 73 74 75 76 77 78 79 80 81 82 83
84 85 86 87 88 89 90 91 92 93 94 95
96 97 98 99 100

Make your own design by connecting the dots.

Designs will vary.

105

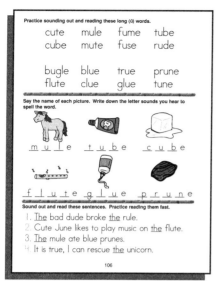

Practice sounding out and reading these long (ū) words.

cute	mule	fume	tube
cube	mute	fuse	rude

bugle	blue	true	prune
flute	clue	glue	tune

Say the name of each picture. Write down the letter sounds you hear to spell the word.

m u <u>l</u> e   t u <u>b</u> e   <u>c</u> u <u>b</u> e

<u>f</u> <u>l</u> u t e   <u>g</u> <u>l</u> u e   <u>p</u> <u>r</u> u <u>n</u> e

Sound out and read these sentences. Practice reading them fast.

1. <u>The</u> bad dude broke <u>the</u> rule.
2. Cute June likes to play music on <u>the</u> flute.
3. <u>The</u> mule ate blue prunes.
4. It is true, I can rescue <u>the</u> unicorn.

106

Page 106